INSPIRATIONAL SPORTS STORIES FOR YOUNG READERS

HOW 12 WORLD-CLASS ATHLETES OVERCAME CHALLENGES AND ROSE TO THE TOP

Kurt Taylor

CONTENTS

INTRODUCTION

It is often said sports are one of the greatest ways to learn life lessons. Through your participation in sports, you learn important skills like dedication, the value of hard work, and perseverance. You learn how to win and lose with grace, and how to interact with teammates to create a better community. There is a reason so many former athletes say that sports helped them learn how to survive in this world.

What makes those skills easier to learn is that you are actually going through the process at the moment. When you win a game, you feel joy and excitement when the final whistle blows. When you lose, disappointment and frustration take hold at the same time. You learn how to use losses as motivating factors and how nice it feels to see your hard work pay off in a championship. You see in real-time how your one pass led to your teammate scoring, or how your hustle helped stop the other team from scoring.

This book isn't going to give you the same real-time feedback, but it will teach you the same valuable life lessons in a different way. Over the next 12 chapters, we're going to cover 12 athletes who took the harder road to their success in sports. You may not be able to relate to all of these 12 athletes, but chances are at least one or two of these stories are going to stick with you. You'll learn how the best athletes in the world dealt with disappointment to rise to the top of their sport. You'll learn how some athletes didn't let their physical limitations stop them from being elite athletes. You'll even learn how some athletes were able to overcome some pretty tough situations to find stability and comfort in the sport they love.

So, over the next 12 chapters, think about how you would react to the situations these athletes found themselves in during their lives. Think about the role that sport plays in your life and what the sports you love mean to you. Many children growing up hoping to score the winning goal or land that perfect 10 from the judges, but only a special few can live out those dreams. What common themes do you see from these athletes that allowed them to become the stars they are today? What lessons can you learn from how these people handled the same situations you may very well find yourself in today or in the future?

We hope this book serves as an inspiration to you to go live out your dreams to the best of your ability. Learn from these 12 stars to figure out how to make your dreams come true and find your true happiness.

JIM ABBOTT

It's not often you see an athlete with a body that isn't in pristine condition. Athletes are known for their strong muscles and bodies that are in peak physical conditioning. Yet few people have the mental strength and perseverance of Jim Abbott.

Abbott was born with a partially-formed right arm, which in theory should have ruled out a lot of sports from his career choices - certainly any sport that would require him to throw a ball. Yet Abbott played in the major leagues, doing so for 10 years, making 254 starts and 263 appearances as a pitcher, the kind of position you wouldn't expect from someone with just one fully-formed arm. So, just how did Jim Abbott find baseball and become the most iconic athlete with a major disability?

Jim Abbott was born on September 19, 1967, in Flint, Michigan to two teenagers, Mike and Kathy Abbott. It certainly wasn't ideal circumstances for either the new parents or the newborn, but Mike and Kathy showed the same resolve in raising Jim while finishing college as he would later show in making it to the major leagues. As Jim became more interested in sports, his parents tried to gently direct him to soccer, a sport famous for not needing the use of your hands. Yet everyone in the neighborhood was playing baseball, so that is what Jim Abbott wanted to play.

As any good parent would, Mike would spend hours with Jim working on hand-eye coordination drills to help him accomplish the same motions other kids were doing with two hands. After hours of throwing rubber balls against brick walls and catching the rebounds, Jim eventually began practicing the glove technique that would make him famous. He would elegantly remove his left hand from his glove and then take the ball out of his glove to throw to the base.

Eventually, he decreased the distance between him and the wall, forcing him to utilize the maneuver faster. By the time Jim made it to the majors, he had perfected the dance that became his pitching motion. He would begin with a normal fielder's glove perched on the skin at the end of his right arm as he threw the ball. Once he delivered the ball to the plate, he would slip his left hand into the glove and be prepared to field the ball. When the ball did make its way to Jim, he would remove his glove and cradle it against his chest as he picked the ball out of the webbing and fired it to a teammate.

However, it took a while for Jim to perfect this motion as his parents had a special prosthetic arm made for him when he began school at the age of four. He didn't particularly enjoy his fake arm and he ditched the new limb before even playing a game with it. In his first-ever Little League game, he tossed a no-hitter as an 11-year-old, but it didn't stop the constant stream of doubters that filled Abbott's path to the majors. From Little League through high school and everywhere in between, people assumed Abbott's disability would eventually become a hindrance.

In high school, however, he was playing first base and the outfield when he wasn't pitching, proving himself a more than capable fielder despite his deformity. It didn't even stop Abbott from being a dangerous hitter, with his left arm able to generate tons of power for him. As a senior at Flint Central High School, Abbott bashed seven home runs and batted better than .425 while also winning 10 games with an insanely low 0.75 earned-runs average and averaging more than two strikeouts per inning pitched.

Not only was Abbott successful on the baseball diamond, but his throwing talents also made him a strong starting quarterback on the football team. He threw for more than 600 yards and six touchdowns while starting the final three games of his senior year under center. He also was the team's punter and averaged nearly 38 yards per kick, which is pretty good for a high schooler. At every turn, he found ways to prove people wrong.

Abbott's exploits on the baseball field caught the eye of the Toronto Blue Jays, who drafted the pitcher in the final round of the 1985 MLB Draft out of high school. Wisely, Abbott decided to turn down the $50,000 signing bonus and attend Michigan on a baseball scholarship. It was a major step for Abbott, who hadn't received a lot of recruiting attention due to the skepticism about his disability. But after a successful freshman campaign, Abbott made a name for himself by helping the Wolverines win the Big Ten as a sophomore in 1987 and then pitched a shutout in the NCAA Tournament.

Those performances catapulted Abbott into a new level of stardom as the country came to know his immense talent. In the summer of 1987, Abbott was named to the United States national amateur baseball team and impressed a crowd of more than 50,000 fans with a three-hit complete-game against Cuba in an exhibition game. In the Pan-American Games, Abbott was the flag bearer for the U.S. then won two games without allowing a single run to lead the Americans to a silver medal. He ended up being awarded the Sullivan Award as the nation's best amateur athlete, edging out a standout group of athletes that included future Basketball Hall-of-Famer, David Robinson. Adding to the glory of the 1987 summer, Abbott also won the Golden Spikes Award as the best amateur baseball player over a group that included future big-leaguers Robin Ventura and Ken Griffey Jr.

Yet the summer of 1987 might pale in comparison to what Abbott accomplished in 1988 when he threw a complete game to lead the United States to a win over Japan in the gold medal match of the Olympics. Sure, Abbott was also the first baseball player to be named the Big Ten Male Athlete of the Year that season, but he also was now a gold medalist and a national icon. It wasn't a shock then when he decided to leave Michigan after three years and chase his professional baseball dreams with the California Angels who picked him eighth overall in the 1988 draft.

Perhaps one of the bigger surprises in Abbott's career is that he started in the major leagues, joining the Angels' opening-day rotation in 1989. Only 15 players between the start of the draft in 1965 and Abbott's debut in 1989 had actually started their professional careers in Major League Baseball. And though many believed the Angels keeping Abbott on the opening-day roster was a media stunt, he did finish fifth in Rookie of the Year voting that season with a 12-12 record and a 3.92 ERA with four complete games and two shutouts. After a sophomore slump of sorts in his second year, Abbott put together what became his finest season as a pitcher in 1991. He won 18 games with five complete-game performances with a 2.89 ERA and a career-best 158 strikeouts. Abbott finished third in Cy Young voting that season despite not receiving a first-place vote.

In 1992, Abbott actually had a lower ERA by allowing 2.77 earned runs per nine innings, but the Angels were terrible that season. After the 1992 season, he was traded to the New York Yankees where the best moment of his career occurred. On September 4, 1993, a few weeks shy of his 26th birthday, Abbott threw a no-hitter against the Cleveland Indians. It was a performance filled with plenty of harrowing moments, notably when Felix Fermin's ninth-inning line drive into centerfield was tracked down by Bernie Williams. But more importantly, it put the attention back on Abbott for his baseball abilities, and not the uniqueness of his situation.

However, that success did not last very long for Abbott, who fell back to being an average major leaguer in 1994. The 1995 season was slightly better, but it all came crumbling down for Abbott in 1996 when he went 2-18 with a 7.48 ERA with the Angels. It was a difficult time for Abbott, who was not used to being at such a low on the baseball diamond, and he ended up not playing in 1997 after being released by the Angels. Yet he won all five of his starts with the White Sox in 1998, giving him the motivation to attempt a full comeback in 1999. However, he went just 2-8 before the Brewers cut him, and he eventually decided to retire.

If there was one thing that followed Abbott everywhere during his career, it was the media attention for his disability. He handled every media request with the grace of someone who studied communications at Michigan, and throughout his career, he continued to preach about how much he enjoyed his work in the community. Yet that work also led his boss with the Yankees, owner George Steinbrenner, to criticize him for doing too much with the community and not focusing enough on baseball. There were a lot of reasons, though, that Abbott had such a sharp decline in his career after pitching so well in 1991 and 1992. Most of the popular theories centered on Abbott's disability. He tipped off his pitches because he couldn't shield his grips with a glove. He allowed too many steals because he couldn't conceal his pickoff attempts or field his position as cleanly. The Yankees even created a new glove specifically for Abbott to wear that would fit over his right arm, but it never felt right to the pitcher.

All of those might have played a part, but Abbott never once blamed his disability on the end of his career. He cited the fact he couldn't adjust to losing velocity on his fastball and struggled to throw a consistent off-speed pitch. That is the type of balance most pitchers need in their arsenal, but something Abbott struggled to develop in his career. He finished with 87 wins, 888 strikeouts, and a 4.25 ERA in nearly 1,700 innings on the mound. He threw 31 complete games and six shutouts over 10 seasons in the majors.

"I feel fulfilled. I feel satisfied," Abbott told the media when he announced his retirement in 1999 after being released by Milwaukee. "My career wasn't always great, but it was wonderful. I learned so many lessons and had so many great friends and experiences...My experiences added up, make me feel like I've had a Hall of Fame career."

Abbott now works as a motivational speaker as he tours the country telling his story. He tells all of the classic stories of his no-hitter, his football triumphs, and so much more that went into his life. He wanted his best to help others in the retirement phase of his life, and he continues to do that with his speaking and charity work. He teaches about the need to ADAPT (Adjustability, Determination, Accountability, Perseverance, and Trust) and how that word has taken on a new meaning in his life as he's grown older.

From the hard work, it took to learn how to play baseball with one arm to the mental strength it took to come back after the worst parts of his career. From the fact he took full ownership of his mistakes in his career to the moments, he needed to believe in himself to accomplish the magical moments of his baseball career. It all came from that word and the mantra that Abbott has used to inspire those around the country.

"I believe that the challenges that we face in life can make us better," Abbott said in a 2010 interview. "I'm not saying that they're easy, and struggle is painful...but if lacking a right hand pushed me in any way, then I have to say I'm thankful for that."

JOSH ALLEN

Every little kid has a dream, and every so often those dreams are well within the realm of possibility. Josh Allen also had a dream as a child and into his adolescence, a very specific path he envisioned for how he would go from a kid in a tiny northern California town to the bright lights of the NFL. Sometimes, though, life throws you curveballs and you need to take a few detours to reach your destination. No one is debating now about whether or not Allen's detours were worthwhile.

Allen's story begins in Firebaugh, California, a blue-collar town just outside of Fresno in the north of the state. He grew up on his grandfather's farm with the expectation that he would be the fourth generation of Allens to farm the California land. His father grew cotton, melons, and wheat, though fields of pistachios and alfalfa also were common in the town. It was the stereotypical one-stoplight town where everyone knew everyone and there weren't any secrets being kept. Except, of course, for Allen.

It was rare for colleges to come calling to small towns like Firebaugh on recruiting visits, and the school couldn't do much to showcase its star. Allen didn't travel to the elite quarterback camps where so many colleges begin their recruiting process. His high school team also didn't make the rounds at camps or 7-on-7 tournaments because so many players - Allen included - were starring for

Firebaugh's other sports teams. Allen was the basketball team's leading scorer and an ace pitcher with a fastball that touched 90 miles per hour. At 6-foot-3, 180 pounds, Allen had the frame of a great quarterback, but he didn't get the recognition.

If there was any theme for Allen throughout his life, it was being underappreciated for his talents. He started as the backup running back in a Pop Warner scrimmage, but he was cut along with his brother from the Dos Palos team. This was even though he played like a boy possessed when he did eventually make it onto the field, leaving an impression on the coaches from the opposing team, Los Banos. His effort and enthusiasm caused the Los Banos coaches to talk amongst themselves about Allen during the game, and that conversation just happened to be close enough to Josh's dad, Joel, that when Josh was cut from the Dos Palos Pop Warner team, he found a new home pretty quickly.

Los Banos was 45 minutes away from Firebaugh, which didn't have enough kids for its own Pop Warner program, and the Allens would drive past Dos Palos on the way to practice and games. It was at this moment that Allen received his first taste of playing quarterback. The Los Banos coaches discussed where to best use Allen but decided to use his athleticism at quarterback instead of running back or safety like he was playing at Dos Palos. The same fanaticism with which he attacked football at an older age was evident even as a nine-year-old as he consistently discussed the game plans and his favorite play calls.

With Allen's football career blossoming, he set his sights up the road at Fresno State, a local Division I school that didn't even play in a power conference. Allen was simply hoping the coaches would see the gem sparkling in its backyard and give him a chance. He attended the school's summer camps and wowed the coaches with his throws, but his recruitment never escalated past the initial talks. In fact, no Division I school offered Allen a scholarship out of high school, though San Diego State was kind enough to let the quarterback on the team as a walk-on. Yet without the promise of playing time, Allen decided he needed a different stage to prove to the rest of the country that he could be an elite quarterback.

That stage was about 65 miles away at Reedley College where one of the assistants was married to one of Allen's cousins. The small-town vibe helped find him an opportunity, but once again Allen was overlooked and wasn't named the starter. In the fourth game of the season, Allen was inserted into the game and ran for four touchdowns. It was a performance good enough that he took over the starting quarterback job and threw for 25 touchdowns and just four interceptions over the final five games. That should have been enough for colleges to be offering Allen scholarships like they were free candy.

Instead, Allen took his recruiting into his own hands and went to the coaches. Every head coach at the FBS level received an email from Allen with a link to his highlight tape. Yet Allen didn't stop there and sent that same email to every offensive coordinator, defensive coordinator, and position coach for the more than 120 FBS schools at the time. After more than 1,000 emails sent out at the end of his year at Reedley, chances were, someone was going to look at the highlight film.

The answer to that lottery was Dave Brown, an assistant coach at Wyoming who was familiar with Allen from his time at Fresno State. He ended up beating the drum for Allen with some of the other Wyoming coaches, and it became clear that this was the quarterback of the Cowboys' future. Wyoming made the hard sell to Allen and his family, promising him that he would be the face of the program for three years. But before Allen could make his final choice, he gave his beloved Fresno State Bulldogs one last chance.

Once again, fortune didn't favor Allen immediately, and he was Wyoming's backup for the 2015 season opener. An injury to the starter, though, gave Allen his chance and he promptly led the Cowboys on a touchdown drive in his first series as the starting quarterback. He probably was about to lead them to a second touchdown when Allen escaped the pocket and was cruising on a 24-yard run. He tried to lower his shoulder and take on a defender, as the scrappy quarterback instinctively does, and broke his collarbone, requiring season-ending surgery.

However, like so many steppingstones on Allen's path, this was yet another blessing in disguise. When Allen arrived at Wyoming, he was big and had all the natural tools to be an elite quarterback. Yet he also wasn't in great shape and many of the natural skills that he had needed to be refined. By the time the start of the 2016 season came around, Allen was now mentally and physically able to harness the immense arm strength and athleticism that made him such a compelling prospect in the first place.

The 2016 season was everything Allen could have dreamed about as he continued his progression into a superstar. By the middle of the year, the once-anonymous quarterback from small-town Firebaugh was a quick riser in mock drafts. Allen could barely get college coaches to respond to him for five years, but six weeks of great football earned him dozens of calls from agents and financial advisors looking to cash in on the 2017 NFL Draft. Even though the 2016 season ended on a sour note with four losses in five games and a back-breaking interception in the season finale, Allen felt ready to turn pro.

Until he didn't.

Those around Allen felt he needed another year at Wyoming to polish off the rough edges that would make him an NFL star. He felt ready to command an NFL huddle at 20 years old with limited experience at the highest levels of the sport. At least, he did until right before the deadline to enter the draft when he began to doubt his decision. Whether it was one last call from the Wyoming coaches or just a gut feeling in Allen's stomach, he knew that he needed one last ride with the Cowboys.

Every question that teams could have about Allen was answered in 2017 when the quarterback was under the most scrutiny of anyone in the Mountain West. Every game was going to be dissected by NFL scouts trying to determine if Allen was their franchise quarterback, which meant every throw and every decision mattered. Yet whatever happened in that final year at Wyoming was enough to convince one important person that he could play quarterback in the NFL.

When Brandon Beane was doing his research for the 2018 NFL Draft, he had a checklist of what he was looking for in the next quarterback of the Buffalo Bills. Allen continued to check all the boxes from his physical attributes to the attitude he kept about himself. He was confident without being cocky, well-respected among his teammates, coaches, and community, and perhaps most importantly, he was loyal. Allen had chances during his high school career to jump to better opportunities that might have gotten him on college radars. He could have gone to a bigger high school to attract more attention. He could have focused solely on football and let his commitments to baseball and basketball go by the wayside. Instead, he chose to stick by Firebaugh and the community that helped raise him.

The Bills had identified their man, but now they needed to do the draft gymnastics to actually go get him. For the first time in his career, Allen had a team proving just how valuable they believed he could be to them. The quarterback with no college offers out of high school and just one out of junior college impressed Buffalo so much that they traded up in the draft to make sure they could pick Allen.

Of course, being the seventh pick in the draft brought with it new expectations. Allen had reached the pinnacle of his dreams. He was getting the chance to prove he could be the franchise quarterback for an NFL team, now all he had to do was do it. That would be easier said than done, though, as once again Allen found himself named the backup for the Bills' season opener. He would become the starter in the second week, but Allen struggled in his first season in Buffalo and suffered a concussion that kept him out of the lineup for four games.

Allen made improvements ahead of the 2019 season, but once again he left questions about whether or not he could solve the Bills' quarterback woes. He won 10 games and led Buffalo to the playoffs, but many wondered if he had reached his ceiling after making a few critical mistakes in the postseason. He still was completing less than 60 percent of his passes and he was also throwing too many bad interceptions while absorbing massive hits while running. It was an unsustainable formula for the quarterback.

Yet, once again, Allen mustered up the work ethic to prove his detractors wrong and put together an MVP-worthy season in 2020. He finished second in MVP voting that year, leading the Bills to the AFC Championship Game for the first time in more than 25 years. As if it couldn't get any better, Allen raised his game again in 2021 and played near-perfect football in the playoffs yet again, though his defense let him down.

For the first time in his life, no one was questioning Josh Allen's ability or talent. He went from the quarterback no one wanted to the one everyone wants on their team. One reason Allen has been so successful in Buffalo is that the city reminds him so much of Firebaugh with its tight-knit community. Allen himself was the recipient of Buffalo's generosity after his grandmother died and Bills' fans raised more than $1 million for the local children's cancer ward in her honor. All of what made Allen special throughout his life from his loyalty to his work ethic and consistent chip on his shoulder is celebrated and appreciated in Buffalo.

But Allen also has a new attitude toward the game, one that is less about vengeance for the past. He would oftentimes play angry at Wyoming, hoping to destroy the people who doubted him and his abilities. Now, he is simply playing for the love of the game while helping serve as an example of how far perseverance can take you.

"It wasn't about going out there to embarrass people anymore," Allen told *The Buffalo News* after he was drafted. "It was about having fun, and at the same time, I happened to be damn good at it. I developed a platform and help other kids who were in the same situation I had, coming out of high school with no offers, finally getting your one chance and capitalizing."

SIMONE BILES

At some point in Simone Biles' life, it just became a given that she is the greatest gymnast that ever competed. Her adoptive mother dropped the pretense of doubt, making statements about "when" Simone wins compared to the old "if" she wins. Biles herself no longer was nervous about competitions because she thought someone else would beat her; she was more nervous that she wouldn't live up to her own lofty expectations.

None of these facts, though, were known on March 14, 1997, when Biles was born in Columbus, Ohio. It actually would have been quite surprising if anyone could have predicted what Biles would mean to the sport of gymnastics that year. Biles was born to an addict mother and soon Simone and her three siblings were all in foster care in Ohio. Her grandparents eventually came to take them back to Texas, but her biological mother regained custody within less than a year. A few short months later, Biles, three years old at the time, was back in Texas with her younger sister, Adria, while her two other siblings went to live with other families.

Such chaos at home can have a lot of negative impacts on a child, but it never did for Biles, who was young enough that the transition didn't seem out of the ordinary to her. What many would consider a potentially traumatic childhood was actually quite straightforward. She didn't

25

hide the fact the people she called mom and dad were biologically her grandparents, but she also didn't volunteer that information. Adria and Simone were then officially adopted in 2003, which served as an important year in another way for Biles.

Biles was just a normal six-year-old in 2003 when she first encountered gymnastics on a field trip. She couldn't stay still while waiting for her turn on all the apparatus and her natural bounciness radiated to the coaches. The fact she came close to mimicking some of the gymnasts practicing on the other end of the gym was the first sign that perhaps Biles had something special. Aimee Boorman, one of the coaches at Bannon's Gymnastix, sent a letter home with Biles with her impressions, and the rest is history.

To get to history, though, Biles needed to reach an elite level, and with her skill and dedication, that wasn't an issue. She loved going to practice, even begging to go to the gym for practice on days she didn't feel great. Biles found her one true passion and stuck with it, eventually leaving public school to train more often while finishing her studies in homeschool. She blitzed through the various levels within eight years and found herself preparing for her first senior event in 2013, just a decade after first stumbling upon the sport.

That first event in 2013 went about as poorly as an event could go, and any thoughts that she might be a world champion at the end of the year were laughable. Biles said later that she heard every noise at that first event, and it prevented her from focusing on the task at hand - and it was quite obvious. She nearly fell twice on the balance beam, what has become one of her strongest events. Biles actually did slip off the uneven bars and then nearly faceplanted while going through a tumbling pass in her floor exercise routine! An awkward landing on her first vault was enough for Boorman to pull Biles from the event.

Although the meet itself was a disaster for Biles, it was the springboard to the success she would find for most of the next decade in the sport. Her parents set up Biles with a sports psychologist to help her deal with the anxiety of competition. Biles herself was frustrated and disappointed by the performance and found a new level to her training to prove that she would never perform that poorly again. And Martha Karolyi, the legendary coordinator of the United States national team, stepped in with her own critique and advice.

Once it started to click for Biles in 2013, though, it didn't slow down. She became the world champion in 2013 and never let go of her crown in competition. Her plans to enroll at UCLA after the 2016 Olympics and compete for the Bruins were halted by all of her success. She gave up her collegiate eligibility to turn pro, and she became the face of the sport. She became the first woman ever to capture three straight world all-around titles in 2015 then followed that up with a sensational performance at the 2016 Summer Olympics in Brazil. Biles captured five medals in Rio de Janeiro, four of which were gold. She blew away the competition in the all-around and then led the United States to an easy win in the team competition. She then dominated the vault and floor exercise for two more gold medals, then suffered disappointment with a bronze medal in the balance beam.

From 2013 through 2019, Biles competed in five world championships and won the all-around title all five times. Her 25 medals at the world championships are the most for any gymnast, male or female, and her 19 gold medals are also a record by a healthy margin. Just her record gold-medal haul would be enough for the second-most medals of any woman at the world championships. She was as dominant a force as there could be in gymnastics with no one able to come close to topping the 4-foot-8 force that is Simone Biles. She was so ahead of her field that she has four different tricks named after her, and - at the time of writing - no one else has been able to accomplish three of the four tricks during a competition.

If Biles' story had ended with her coronation at the 2019 world championships in Stuttgart, Germany, it would have been worthy of a fairy-tale movie ending. Yet what Biles was accomplishing in the arena paled compared to what she was going through outside of it. In fact, as impressive as Biles was while competing, she was even more stunning when other facts about her life outside of the gym began to become public.

The real trauma in Biles' life did not come from her addict mother or the brief moments she lived in foster care. It wasn't being split up from her other two siblings or moving to a new state at a young age with people she really hadn't met before. Biles showed the mental fortitude to deal with those issues and continue to thrive. What took more courage and more resolve to overcome was the pain inflicted by Dr. Larry Nassar.

Nassar was the team doctor for USA Gymnastics, and Biles confirmed in 2018 that she was one of the many victims of Nassar's reign of terror. The doctor was convicted of dozens of counts of sexual assault as it related to the United States' national gymnastics team. For years, Biles was out there competing and winning medals for the United States as an abuse survivor, and no one knew about it. It was an example of someone being able to persevere through immense pain to perform at an elite level. Although Biles' pain was mental and not physical, her trauma was far worse than any physical injury.

The power of mental health was again a prominent topic for Biles in 2021 when she competed at the postponed 2020 Summer Olympics in Tokyo. It was not a question of whether or not Biles would win, but who would take second. There was no doubt the United States was going to cruise to the gold medal in the team event and Biles was going to cement her Olympic legacy with even more gold medals.

On the first two days of the competition, Biles was not perfect by any means, but there wasn't any doubt that she would turn it on for the finals. She easily qualified for all four event finals and was the clear leader atop the all-around qualification standings. The United States qualified second in the team event, but again, there were never concerns about Biles' ability to perform.

Then during warmups ahead of the team final, Biles failed to complete her vault and instead ended the routine, a full rotation early. It happened again in the actual competition, and her shaky landing was the first sign that something was wrong. Biles quickly jogged out of the arena floor and into the wings. It was only a minute or two later that she withdrew from the team final due to mental health concerns.

The same thing happened two days later with Biles announcing before the individual competition that she would not be defending her gold medal from 2016 in the all-around. One by one, Biles pulled out of the individual event finals as well until on the final day of competition she placed third in the balance beam. That bronze medal tied Biles for the most Olympic medals for any American female gymnast, but it was overshadowed by her mental health concerns.

It turned out that Biles was suffering from the "twisties," a psychological condition that meant she was struggling to orient herself while in the air. It is a common problem for gymnasts in their career, but no one expected it to impact the greatest of all time, who was doing maneuvers far harder than anyone else had ever attempted. Biles has admitted that it was hard to be thrust into the spotlight as a mental health advocate while she was also processing her own issues. However, she also said she wouldn't change her experience for the world, citing the avenue she opened for athletes to openly discuss their own mental health.

In September 2021, she testified to the United States Senate about a government report on the Nassar scandal. In her testimony, Biles eviscerated the FBI for how it handled the investigation and shone a light on how the horrors affected her in Tokyo. She said the fact the Olympics were delayed only increased her suffering as she had to live with the consequences of Nassar's actions for another year. Yet she found an inner strength in making sure the world continued to know about the effects of Nassar's crimes.

"One thing that helped push me each and every day was the goal of not allowing this crisis to be ignored," Biles said in her statement. "I worked incredibly hard to make sure that my presence could help maintain a connection between the failures and the competition at Tokyo 2020. That has proven to be an exceptionally difficult burden for me to carry, particularly when required to travel to Tokyo without the support of any of my family. I am a strong individual and I will persevere."

STEPH CURRY

It's a classic cliché at this point that looks can be deceiving. It's how magicians pull off their best magic tricks, fooling the audience into thinking a gimmick is normal - or sometimes even vice versa. Sometimes once-in-a-generation basketball players look like they are 14 years old even when they're 18 and graduating high school. And sometimes, pure talent and grit can overcome whatever physical picture someone is imagining on the recruiting trail.

Stephen Curry was born on March 14, 1988, and his destiny to be a professional athlete was almost preordained. He is the son of Dell and Sonya Curry, both of whom played sports at Virginia Tech where they met on Sonya's recruiting visit. Dell was the superstar basketball player who would later have a 16-year NBA career that brought the younger Curry around the country. Sonya was a volleyball star who later became an educator and now runs a school in western North Carolina.

Although he was born in Akron, Ohio while his father played for the Cleveland Cavaliers, Steph Curry became a legend in Charlotte, North Carolina. When his dad was playing for the Charlotte Hornets, Steph and his younger brother, Seth, would tag along with their father. Both of them would participate in shootaround and warmups with the team before taking their seats for the actual game. It was from those moments that the legend of Steph Curry first began to percolate. He wasn't just an ordinary kid taking warmups with his dad and a bunch of other professional athletes; he was a prodigy of sorts with a shot that was on its way to becoming lethal to nets around the United States.

When Dell finished his career with three seasons with the Toronto Raptors, Steph moved to Canada and showed a new country what he could do. He led his school team from Queensway Christian College to an unbeaten championship season. He took his club team to an Ontario provincial championship with a 33-4 record that included matchups against teams led by future NBA players Cory Joseph and Kelly Olynyk. Curry may have been undersized and looked a lot younger than his true age, but there was never doubting his skill.

At least, that was the thought when he entered Charlotte Christian School as a 5-foot-8, 125-pound freshman. Curry hit a growth spurt and built his muscle a tad to graduate high school at 6-foot-1, 160 pounds, but that was not considered nearly big enough to be a successful player at a big-time program. Never mind his tremendous scoring acumen or the fact his teams won everywhere he went. They ignored the fact he rarely missed when he was open, and how he found ways to create his own shot with the tiniest amount of space. All that mattered was, as one recruiting service leader put it, that Curry was "way over his head physically."

Curry may not have had the physical strength of some of the other players in his class, but that didn't stop him from having a singular goal. He wanted to follow in his father's footsteps at Virginia Tech and become a star for the Hokies. The Virginia Tech coach at the time, Seth Greenberg, wasn't willing to play the legacy game and no major school offered Curry a scholarship opportunity. The best chance Curry had was to walk on at Virginia Tech and then sit out a year as a redshirt player to prove his worth. There was no benching the competitive Curry, however, so he needed a new plan.

While all of the bigger schools in the nation ignored Curry's talents, there was one man not too far away from Charlotte that certainly believed in the youngster. Bob McKillop first saw Steph Curry when Curry was 10 years old and teammates with McKillop's son Brendan on a baseball team. It was the longtime Davidson College coach's first glimpse into what type of athlete Curry could be. He didn't see Curry play basketball until his freshman year at Charlotte Christian, and it became clear that this was the person McKillop wanted to build his program around.

The next year, McKillop began the full-court press for Curry in hopes of being in a perfect position if the bigger schools continued to overlook Curry. As the calendar moved closer to November 2005 when Curry was set to sign his National Letter of Intent, Davidson's position kept improving. The school was roughly 30 miles from Curry's high school, had a legendary coach in McKillop, and there was plenty of playing time for the offering. It wasn't the bright lights of the ACC in Blacksburg, Virginia, but it had everything else Curry could have wanted in a school.

As the time for a decision drew near, McKillop continued to express the same message that Davidson would build around Curry. There was never a doubt he was going to be the focal point for the Wildcats, the star around which Davidson would hope to make some noise in the NCAA Tournament. As soon as Curry signed the dotted line on his NLI, McKillop began boasting to boosters about Curry's talent, telling them to just wait until they saw him on the court.

All of the hype behind the scenes for Curry at Davidson fell flat in his first game for the Wildcats. He was the team's starting point guard as a freshman for the season opener, and Curry's performance was about as bad as it could get. He committed eight turnovers in the first half and had 13 total for the game, a fact erased by his 15 points in a

Davidson victory. Halftime of that opener against Eastern Michigan might have been the only time McKillop had to think about benching his budding superstar due to nerves or performance issues.

After surviving opening night, Curry had a weight lifted off his shoulders as he had his first chance to prove to the world what they missed. Davidson's second game of the 2006 season was against Michigan from the mighty Big Ten. The Wildcats lost that game by 10 points, but no one was talking about that result after the game. The bigger story was the local freshman who dropped 32 points and made seven of his 10 three-point attempts in only his second Division I game. Curry lighting up the scoresheet became a common occurrence for Davidson during that 2006-07 season during which he led all freshmen in the nation with 21.5 points per game.

Davidson won 29 games that season and advanced to the NCAA Tournament as a 13 seed. Curry scored 30 points in a first-round loss to Maryland as an appetizer for what was to come in 2007-08. Once again, the start of the season did not spoil the ending of the story as Davidson struggled mightily with a 3-6 record against Division I opponents to open the year. It didn't help that McKillop had scheduled three of the 'bluest bloods' in the sport - Duke, North Carolina, and UCLA - in that stretch, but Curry held his own with 24 points against the Tar Heels and 20 against the Blue Devils. After losing right before Christmas in North Carolina State despite 29 points from Curry, the Wildcats flipped the switch. They won 25 straight games, which included capping off a perfect 20-0 run in the Southern Conference and then blitzing through the three games at the SoCon Tournament. However, that run only left Davidson at 22 consecutive wins as it entered the NCAA Tournament as a No. 10 seed.

The world was officially introduced to Steph Curry on March 21, 2008, when Davidson faced off with perennial power Gonzaga in the first round of the NCAA Tournament. Curry scored an astounding 40 points on 63.6 percent shooting to lead the Wildcats to their first NCAA Tournament victory in nearly 40 years in what was future Hall-of-Fame coach Lefty Driesell's final season at the school. Two days later, Curry was limited to just 30 points on a much more difficult shooting night to lead Davidson to the Sweet 16 with a win over second-seeded Georgetown.

Davidson won those first two games by a combined 10 points, but it was a much different story against Wisconsin in the third game. Curry continued to toy with the Badgers in that game with 33 points in a 17-point Davidson victory to set up a matchup with No. 1 Kansas in the regional final. What was perhaps most impressive about Curry's performance against Wisconsin is that it came against a defense known for harassing shooters and frustrating some of the best in the sport to miss open shots. Even with Wisconsin's best defender hounding him for 40 minutes, Curry stayed patient and didn't force anything. If the Badgers wanted to take him out of the game, it would open the door for his teammates, notably Jason Richards who dished out 13 assists.

By the time Davidson took the court on March 30, 2008, in Detroit against Kansas, everyone knew Curry's name. He had become the story of the tournament in leading a small school from western North Carolina to the Elite Eight against one of the biggest brands in the sport. For 40 minutes, the two teams locked horns and competed. Curry would miss 12 of his 16 attempts from behind the arc, but he did finish with 25 points. Unfortunately for him and the Wildcats, that was two points too few as Davidson's run was ended by the eventual national champions.

Once the emotions settled from the tough loss, it became obvious to most that Curry was ready for the NBA. Curry had averaged nearly 26 points per game, and he'd proved during the tournament run that he was capable of competing against the best players in the country. It certainly was a consideration for Curry and his family, but he felt he had something to prove as a point guard, so he decided on one more year at Davidson. There was no fairy-tale ending for Curry with the Wildcats in 2008-09 as Davidson was upset in the conference tournament and then bowed out in the second round of the NIT. Curry did lead the nation with 28.6 points per game, but he also averaged almost six assists per game with the ball in his hands more.

Curry didn't have to wait too long to hear his name called in the 2009 NBA Draft, though many will argue he was drafted too low at No. 7 overall. But he was there for the Golden State Warriors, and they wasted no time in picking him and making him the anchor of their future plans. The problem was it took the Warriors a bit to actually put those plans into motion as for the first time in a long time, Curry was starring for a team that didn't have success. He averaged 17.5 points per game as a rookie then 18.6 points in his second year before he missed most of the 2011-12 season with foot injuries.

Yet when the 2012-13 season began, Curry once again had doubters to disprove thanks to his new contract. Many critics were skeptical of the Warriors investing in Curry after the injuries, especially when the team had four straight losing seasons and not a lot of hope that it would change soon. Instead, though, the Warriors actually made the playoffs that year behind Curry averaging nearly 23 points per game and earning his first All-Star nod. Golden State

41

bowed out in the second round that season then fell in the first round the following year with Curry averaging 24 points per game.

That was the backdrop for the 2014-15 season in which everyone appreciated Curry for his skill but wasn't convinced of his championship pedigree. Yet Curry led Golden State to the top seed in the Western Conference that year to earn his first MVP award after averaging 23.8 points and 7.7 assists per game while shooting 48 percent from the floor. That, of course, was an award for his regular-season accomplishments; his championship validation came when he helped Golden State take down the Cavaliers for the Warriors' first title in 40 years.

Curry was even better the following year while leading the league with 30.1 points and 2.1 steals per game in addition to his 50 percent shooting percentage. That included Curry making more than 45 percent of his three-pointers, the best percentage he's shot in a season that he played at least 30 games. It culminated in a record-breaking 73-win regular season and a heartbreaking loss to Cleveland in the NBA Finals. Golden State would go on to win the next two NBA Finals and then lose in an injury-plagued series to Toronto in 2018-19, which put a new type of pressure on Curry.

The five straight trips to the NBA Finals clearly took a toll on the Warriors as most of their best players were lost for the 2019-20 season due to injury. The bad luck hit Curry as well after he broke his hand four games into the season and then missed more than three months before returning for what ultimately became the team's final game of the season in March. Golden State predictably struggled without their star and was the worst team in the NBA when the pandemic shut down the league. When Curry came back the following year, he led the league in scoring with 32 points per game, but the team's success was again missing as the Warriors missed the playoffs.

By the time the 2021-22 season rolled around, Curry was already among the pantheon of great scorers, but he still had his share of detractors. They complained that he hadn't led a team to a title himself, requiring the help of some talented teammates to win his previous three championships. He put all that noise to rest that year, dragging the Warriors to yet another NBA championship as the Western Conference Finals and NBA Finals MVPs. He averaged 25.5 points and 6.3 assists per game in the regular season then turned up the volume with 27.4 points and six assists per game in the playoffs.

"I hear all the narratives," Curry said after finishing off Boston to win the title in June 2022. "You hear everything about what we [as a team] are and what we aren't, and what I am as a player and what I'm not...The fact that when we started this season, the conversations about who we were as a team and what we were capable of, clearly remember some experts and talking heads putting up the big zero of how many championships we would have going forward because of everything that we went through. So, we hear all that, and you carry it all and you try to maintain your purpose, not let it distract you, but you carry that weight and to get here, it all comes out. It's special."

BETHANY HAMILTON

Bethany Hamilton was born to be in the water. Like so many people who know exactly what they want to do from a young age, it was easy to see Hamilton belonged in the ocean. She was born on February 8, 1990, in Hawaii, which already positioned her to be a lover of water. Her parents were avid surfers, too, and she and her brothers were quickly on surfboards learning to handle the waves. By the age of three, Hamilton knew how to surf, and her first surfing competition came when she was eight years old.

When Hamilton decided to surf competitively, she also shifted from her normal school routine and moved to homeschool. It would give her more flexibility to surf and practice without the time commitments of being in school while the sun shone brightly on the Hawaiian beaches. It became increasingly obvious that Bethany was going to surpass the talents of the rest of her family, all of whom are still excellent recreational surfers. Bethany signed her first sponsorship deal before she turned 10 and she earned second place in the National Scholastic Surfing Association's national championships in July 2003.

At the moment of that triumph at the age of 13, no one could have predicted how much Bethany's life was about to change. Four months after standing high as the runner-up for the NSSA event, Hamilton was surfing with her best friend, Alana, and Alana's dad on an otherwise typical

Halloween day. While paddling out to the waves, Hamilton was attacked by a tiger shark with a bite so clean that it took off her left arm just below the shoulder. The shock of the moment didn't really hit Bethany until she was being dragged to shore as she fell in and out of consciousness while the blood poured out of her. It is estimated that she lost about two thirds/3 of her blood that day, but her spirit and faith never left her.

While Bethany was surfing with her friend that day, her father was being prepped for minor knee surgery when he was told that the operation needed to be delayed due to an emergency. All he was told was that there'd been a shark attack on a girl at Makua Beach, and he immediately knew the only two people it could have been. As soon as he saw the blonde hair on the girl on the gurney, he knew it was Bethany who had been attacked. Meanwhile, Bethany's mother was racing toward the hospital behind the ambulance, going fast enough that she was pulled over by local police. A quick call from the ambulance cleared up the confusion, but it was a scary moment for everyone around Bethany.

At no point did it feel to Bethany that her surfing career had ended or that she would never return to the water. She actually was waiting with bated breath for the doctors to give her the all-clear to return to the ocean and get back on a surfboard. Before she did return, though, she faced the demon that took her arm from her thanks to a local fisherman who caught the shark. While staring down the jaw of the shark, the powerful bones that ripped off her arm, Hamilton just asked for some teeth for a necklace she wanted to make and slept in her car ride back to her home with her father.

It took Hamilton just 26 days to return to surfing after her arm was torn off as she tried to discover a new normal. As she would say several times, her love of the ocean and her passion for surfing outweighed any lingering fear she had about sharks. She attempted to surf on a modified longer board to help with her balance and struggled to get up on her first two attempts. She made it on the board for her third attempt and rode the wave to the shore, but it didn't take long for her to return to the shortboard.

Two months after getting back on a surfboard, Hamilton actually competed again and finished fifth in a regional event with the NSSA. In the summer of 2004, Hamilton took fifth place in the national competition, proving to everyone that she still had a long, fruitful career ahead of her.

All of the potentials that Hamilton showcased in her youth came together in 2005 when she won the NSSA national championship for girls 18 years old and younger. She won the O'Neill Island Girl Junior Pro that year as well, proving she was more than capable of competing at the highest level no matter how many arms she had at her disposal.

It wasn't until 2008 that Hamilton tried to go pro by competing in the Association of Surfing Pros' qualifying series. Now called the World Surf League, Hamilton had to finish inside the top three of the series to earn a spot in the professional circuit. Her goal at the age of 18 was simply to finish inside the top 30 of the second-tier competition, but she actually finished in 14th. She finished in 14th place again in 2009, but she earned a wildcard invitation to Gidget Pro at Sunset Beach in Hawaii for her first chance to surf at an elite event. She finished in 13th place in the event to set up a strong close to the year on the waves.

Hamilton surfed to a third-place finish at the Rio Surf Invitational then finished second in the World Junior Championships that were being held in Australia. Over the coming years, Hamilton didn't qualify for a full-time spot on the WSL tour, but she made the most of her wildcard opportunities in events. As the first female to compete in the Rip Curl Cup, Hamilton won her first heat and then was eliminated in the quarterfinals in 2012. She won the Surf N Sea Pipeline Pro in 2014 for her first professional victory and added a third-place finish in the 2016 Fiji Women's Pro, her best finish on the WSL tour. That performance in Fiji was arguably the pinnacle of Hamilton's career because she took down a six-time world champion and the top-ranked surfer in the world during that event.

After 2016, Hamilton took time off from competing to raise her family with her husband, Adam. In 2020, Hamilton attempted to make her comeback and qualify for the WSL but came up short in her attempts. Her goal to be a professional surfer has certainly taken a backseat to family commitments, but her perseverance cannot be questioned. She wrote an autobiography about her experiences after returning to surfing in 2004 and that later was turned into a movie.

Hamilton has mostly turned her attention now to motivational speaking and writing motivational materials, including a book and a life coach course. However, her competitive spirit is still within her as she is still an active professional on the scene. She might be limiting her events and not at the greatest heights, but she is still continuing to prove people wrong daily.

"Looking in hindsight, I see all the beauty and good that's come from the loss of my arm that I wouldn't change life to be how I think it should be, but rather just embracing life as it is," Hamilton told CNN in 2019.

LEBRON JAMES

Oftentimes, an athlete is so dominant and so talented you can only assume they were born to play that sport. From the moment he stepped on a basketball court, it felt like LeBron James was destined for NBA stardom as he dominated every level of basketball along the way. What people forget is there are moments before an athlete finds their sport where the path may change. That certainly was the case for LeBron, who had several opportunities to see his NBA career derailed before he even played an organized game of basketball.

It all began for James on December 30, 1984, in Akron, Ohio when he was born to a 16-year-old mother. Gloria James did her best growing up to support LeBron, especially with his father out of the picture due to an extensive criminal history. As she worked to keep food on the table, the two of them moved quite a bit around Akron while she attempted to find steadier employment. They would bounce from house to house, trying to find a place to sleep for a few nights with friends and family.

The constant movement affected LeBron's education as he would end up living far away from school. In fourth grade alone, James missed 80 days of school, which is nearly half of the school year. When he did show up, his teachers raved about his intelligence and work ethic, but without consistent transport to school, it was difficult for him to make the daily commitment to his education. He ended up finding a stable living situation with his football coach, Bruce Kelker, who was looking for players for his football team and was tipped off to James' athletic talent.

After football ended in his fifth-grade year, LeBron met Frank Walker and his family. Gloria made the difficult choice to allow LeBron to move in with the Walker family, and it was Frank who ended up really teaching LeBron about basketball and not just using his natural athleticism. When he first met Walker, James lost a game of one-on-one to one of Walker's sons by the score of 21-7. A few months later, James was a completely different player, dominating games by scoring with both hands and dribbling more consistently.

His passion for football never died within LeBron, but it became clear early on that basketball was going to be his true calling. Some may argue LeBron James could have become synonymous with the greatest receivers of all time given his all-state performances in high school. However, it was impossible to deny the potential and ability LeBron showed on the basketball court.

It was in eighth grade when James' talent and potential were first put on full display. It was a simple student versus faculty-basketball game at Riedinger Middle School, and as one would expect, the teachers were heavy favorites. Then again, they'd never had to compete against a player of James' caliber before. The students were actually pulling away when James found himself on a fastbreak alone and did the unthinkable for a 14-year-old - he dunked the ball! The crowd in the gym erupted and one might argue it was the coronation for the man later dubbed "King James."

James was also a dominant force in the AAU circuit with the Northeast Ohio Shooting Stars and their version of the Fab Four. The group consisted of James, Dru Joyce III, and Sian Cotton before Willie McGee rounded out the foursome a year later. With just James, Joyce, and Cotton, the Shooting Stars did the unthinkable and qualified for the national tournament in Florida. Even more remarkable, they finished in ninth place of the 64 teams in a tournament Coach Joyce wasn't even sure he wanted to enter because of the driving distance! McGee then joined the team, and their relationship grew strong enough that they all decided to play high school basketball together at St. Vincent - St. Mary High School.

That AAU team was coached by Joyce's father, Dru Joyce II, who also played a critical role in James' development. Joyce was the one who discovered James at a local gym and invited him to play for the Shooting Stars, and he followed the foursome to St. Vincent-St. Mary as an assistant coach for two years. The Fighting Irish won the state championship in both 1999-2000 and 2000-01, setting up what could have been a dynasty. However, head coach Keith Dambrot left the school after those two seasons to jump back into the college coaching ranks. Joyce II took over and that third year was a disaster for St. Vincent-St. Mary.

The Fighting Irish didn't win the state championship in 2001-02 as the media attention around LeBron hit a frenzy. *ESPN The Magazine* dubbed James "The Chosen One" in its NEXT issue, and the attention from Nike and other major apparel companies was totally crazy. In an era when 18-year-olds could still enter the NBA Draft, the rumors were already circulating that James would skip college and go directly to the pros. That second title turned James from a basketball phenom into a celebrity with people selling tickets to his games for $50 and opponents asking for a postgame autograph.

The attention didn't slow down for his senior season, especially after James sued the NBA in an attempt to become eligible for the 2002 draft. That petition was unsuccessful, but James had a far more important appeal go in his favor. All of the hype around James during his senior year meant he was the most-watched high school player in the country, if not the most-watched basketball player. St. Vincent - St. Mary played in several showcase games on national television against other powerhouse programs, and every game that year was streamed by Time Warner Cable as a pay-per-view. Everyone wanted to watch LeBron James play basketball and be associated with him somewhat.

That ultimately led to some trouble for James and his family when gifts started to arrive. Gloria bought LeBron a Hummer using his future earnings as collateral for the loan, and the Ohio High School Athletic Association had to review it if violated their policy. What certainly deemed James ineligible, were two throwback jerseys he received as gifts from a local store whose value exceeded the allowable limit in the state. James eventually appealed that suspension and returned to lead the Fighting Irish to yet another state title, however, the team was forced to vacate a win from earlier in the season, putting a blemish on an otherwise perfect record.

With a state title - and the national title from *USA Today* as the top-ranked team in the country - James was free to pursue his professional career in earnest. There was never a question of whether or not James would be the first pick in the 2003 NBA Draft, but it remained to be seen just who would hold the top selection.

As fate would have it, the hometown Cleveland Cavaliers won the draft lottery that year and the opportunity to draft the three-time Ohio Mr. Basketball. It was the perfect situation for LeBron, whose roots in the community and love for Northeast Ohio made him the ideal face of the franchise. He scored 25 points in his first professional game, the most by anyone who made their NBA debut straight out of high school, he then went on to win the Rookie of the Year as well. He became just the third first-year player to average 20 points, five rebounds, and five assists in his first season.

The 20.9 points he averaged as a rookie was the only time that he's ever averaged less than 25 points per game in his NBA career. James would end up spending the first seven seasons of his career with the Cavaliers and leading the team to the NBA Finals for the first time in franchise history in 2006-07. Cleveland may have been swept by San Antonio in those Finals, but there was tremendous optimism for what the future held for the team. James would lead the league in scoring in 2007-08, but Cleveland was knocked out in the conference semifinals. LeBron was the league MVP in 2008-09 and then again, the following year, but the playoff results were similar, losing in the conference finals and then conference semifinals.

There was growing tension between James and Cavaliers ownership during that 2009-10 season, and the loss to Boston in the conference semifinals was the last straw. For nearly two decades, LeBron had been the toast of Northeast

Ohio and beloved by everyone in the state for what he did at St. Vincent - St. Mary and then with the Cavaliers. No one expected James to ever leave home, especially not before he delivered the championship-starved city the title they so desperately desired.

Then came July 8, 2010.

If there was a moment when LeBron James turned into the villain of his own story, it was that night in Greenwich, Connecticut. For the first week in July, James was a free agent and heard pitches from several teams around the league. On July 8, he decided to announce his decision on ESPN in a television special appropriately named, "The Decision." LeBron officially announced he was signing with the Miami Heat that night and was universally critiqued for the delivery of his decision and the actual choice he made. By this point, the comparisons to Michael Jordan were unavoidable, but the notion of leaving to join two other stars as a "Big Three" was simply unheard of.

James spent four seasons with the Heat, advancing to the NBA Finals in all four years and winning his first two championships. He added two more NBA MVP awards and was named the MVP of the Finals in both victories as well. Yet James' career was still very much incomplete, so he decided to return home, penning a touching tribute to Cleveland in *Sports Illustrated* to announce his decision.

Similar to his time in Miami, James led his team to the NBA Finals in all four years he played with the Cavaliers in his second stint. He won just one of those four trips, but it was a special championship indeed. Not only was it Cleveland's first sports championship in 52 years, but the Cavaliers accomplished it by rallying from down 3-1 in the series and having to face elimination in each of the final three games. The fact James sealed the title with what is affectionately known as "The Block" only added to the celebrations that night.

LeBron added a fourth title with the Lakers in 2019-20, in what was his ninth consecutive appearance in the NBA Finals with three different franchises. On the face of it, James' on-court accomplishments are unmistakable. He's a four-time league MVP, a four-time NBA Finals MVP, an 18-time All-Star, and he made the all-defensive team six times. He's averaged more than 27 points, 7.5 rebounds, and 7.4 assists per game over a career spanning 19 seasons through the end of 2021-22.

No one debates whether or not LeBron James is one of the best to ever play and no one questions what he's done for his community. As much as LeBron might have broken people's hearts by leaving the Cavaliers twice, his philanthropic work in the Akron area is legendary. At the very least, James is acutely aware of just how quickly he could have turned into a statistic and been an unknown adult from Akron with untapped potential on the basketball court.

"Growing up in the inner city, the numbers are always stacked up against you," James told ESPN in 2018 at the opening of his new school in Ohio. "So, you didn't really know what was possible. I think what happened for me was that I got some mentors and little league coaches and some teachers that I kind of started to believe in. And they started to make my dreams feel like they could actually become a reality.

"If it wasn't for meeting these families and meeting these people, then I would never have even gotten to a point where you guys know who I am today as the basketball player, but more importantly, the guy who's giving back to his community. I just give a lot of credit and a lot of thanks to my mentorship and to the people who were just there for me."

LIONEL MESSI

It is often difficult to pick out exactly which part of Lionel Messi's path to being the best soccer player in the world was more improbable. Was it the fact he nearly was denied from playing the sport by his mother? His physical limitations that required medical assistance? Or the fact he had to travel across the Atlantic Ocean to fulfill his dream. Messi has dominated the soccer world since making his professional debut in 2004 for FC Barcelona, but nothing about his story until that moment was normal.

Lionel Messi was born June 24, 1987, in Rosario, Argentina, a year that would become very important for the locals in short order. Messi was always with a soccer ball in some form for most of his early youth, and his skills were discovered at five years old by a local coach. Salvador Aparicio approached Celia Messi about young Lionel playing for Club Grandoli, the club where his two older brothers played, and she declined. She claimed he was too small and too unskilled to participate, but Messi's grandmother stepped in and told Celia to let him play.

Within a year, Messi's talent was too apparent to ignore, and he was signed by the local professional club in Rosario, Newell's Old Boys. It was there that Messi teamed up with the rest of the 1987-born children, a group that would later be termed "Máquina '87" or Machine '87. The team would dominate the local competition and it felt like the club had stumbled upon the next nucleus of the team's success once the boys matured and developed. The problem was everyone began to develop and mature at a much faster rate than Lionel Messi.

For most of the four years Messi played with Newell's Old Boys, the fact he was smaller than the rest of the group wasn't an issue. His oversized talent made his shorter frame irrelevant, but in December 1996, the story changed. All of a sudden, the club's directors wanted to run some tests on Lionel with Dr. Diego Schwarzstein, a leading endocrinologist in the area. After a year of tests to home in on exactly what was causing the slow growth, Schwarzstein determined Messi was not producing nearly enough human growth hormone, and he would need injections to supplement his body's production.

It was a fairly simple and routine solution, but the costs for the treatment were extraordinary. The injections cost around $1,500 each month, the type of money the Messis just didn't have to spend on the medication. For the first few months in Argentina, insurance, Newell's Old Boys, and the steel company where Messi's father, Jorge, worked covered the costs. Yet the economy started to collapse in Argentina and there simply wasn't enough to pay for the injections anymore. Newell's Old Boys was unable to shoulder more of the economic load, so Jorge Messi went on the lookout for solutions for his son in 1999.

Jorge was fortunate that his son's big break actually came to Argentina instead. A few people with ties to FC Barcelona saw Messi playing for Newell's Old Boys and suggested the Spanish club give him a tryout. After some intense back-and-forth, Messi was granted a trial with the club in 2000 at the age of 13. It was a rarity for the club to audition a player from outside of Europe, especially one as young as Messi. Even after Messi impressed the club's director, Carlos Rexach, and convinced him that the club needed to sign the Argentinian, the Messis still had to play a waiting game.

Eventually, the time had come for Barcelona to decide on Messi as the family had been in Spain for nearly a month. Jorge gave Rexach and the club an ultimatum: sign my son to a contract or we're leaving. Pressed for time, Rexach used the only paper product at his disposal, a napkin, to write out the terms of the deal. Barcelona would find a job for Jorge and would pay for Lionel's hormone treatment, and Rexach overruled the skeptics in the club hierarchy to sign Messi on the most famous napkin in soccer history.

Of course, Lionel Messi's transition from Argentina to Spain was a difficult one. His entire family was able to join him originally, but his mother and siblings returned home after a year, leaving just Lionel and Jorge in Barcelona. Meanwhile, Messi was unable to play in most of Barcelona's youth games as a foreigner, so he was limited to just competition within Catalonia. The fact he also was injured during that first year didn't help matters for the naturally shy Messi. He was so shy that his teammates called him "el mudo" or "the mute one" because he did not interact or speak with his teammates much.

Messi had the option to return to Argentina with his mother and siblings, but he saw the opportunity being presented to him in Barcelona. And once he got on the field for Barcelona, his meteoric rise through the club was unstoppable. At the age of 16, he was finally able to play for most of the Barcelona teams, and he made appearances for five different branches of the club, including the first team. It was just a friendly against FC Porto from Portugal with most of the other first-team players on international duty, but it was an important step, nonetheless. From that November 2003 debut, it was only a year before Messi made a competitive appearance for the first team.

In October 2004, Messi was a substitute for the final 10 minutes of a La Liga match against Espanyol. At 17 years old, he became the youngest player to appear for Barcelona in nearly a century. Although he didn't shine in those first minutes on the field, that 2004-05 season proved to be the last time anyone questioned Messi's spot on the first-team roster. He ended the season with one goal in nine appearances for the first team, scoring on May 1, 2005, against Albacete in a preview of what Barcelona fans would come to expect for the next 16 years.

Messi scored eight goals in 25 appearances the next season, and then 17 in 2006-07, the first time he appeared in at least half of Barcelona's league matches. By the end of the 2020-21 season, Messi had scored 672 goals in 778 total games for the club, surpassing every conceivable record for Barcelona and La Liga as a whole. He was just as spectacular in the biggest moments as well with 120 goals in 149 games in European competitions.

The Argentinian was also the catalyst of a period of unprecedented success for the club. Before Messi made his competitive debut for the club, Barcelona had gone five long years without a trophy. In 17 seasons with Messi on the squad, Barcelona won La Liga a staggering 10 times and added seven Copa del Rey trophies. The club was European champions four times as winners of the Champions League in addition to five other appearances in the Champions League semifinals. In total, Barcelona won 35 trophies with Messi on the roster, the most trophies won by a player at a single club in world history.

On an individual level, Messi turned into the best player on the planet with very few rivals. He was named the world player of the year by winning the Ballon D'Or seven times in a 13-year stretch with five runner-up finishes in that span. He led the continent in goal-scoring six times in a 11-year period, setting the record for most goals in a calendar year with 96 in 2012, the same year he scored a record 79 goals in competitive matches for Barcelona. It was also the back half of Messi's record-setting 2011-12 season when he scored 73 total goals for the club.

It wasn't a bad ending for a kid who arrived in Spain at 4-foot-7 while stabbing injections into his leg every day. Messi never became the biggest or strongest player in the world, but he did grow a full foot to 5-foot-7, surpassing Argentinian legend Diego Maradona. The man who started off as "the mute one" ended up being a very vocal leader of Barcelona's success, even if most of that talking happened behind closed doors and away from the public.

"I always thought I wanted to play professionally, and I always knew that to do that I'd have to make a lot of sacrifices," Messi said in an interview. "I made sacrifices by leaving Argentina, leaving my family to start a new life. I changed my friends and my people. Everything. But everything I did, I did for football, to achieve my dream."

PELÉ

In many ways, the story of Pelé is no different than so many of the superstars of the 1960s and 1970s. In an era before specialized training and elite resources, all most players had at their disposal was a ball and some space. Yet sometimes not even a ball or a playing field was guaranteed, and whatever you could scrounge up to make the game as lifelike as possible was what you used. Many of those players didn't end up becoming the greatest player of all time; the others are people like Pelé.

He was born Edson Arantes do Nascimento on October 23, 1940, in Brazil and found himself with several nicknames before Pelé stuck. To his family, he was always Dico, the nickname he acquired as a young boy. Yet to pretty much anyone else who has ever seen or heard of his greatness, he is simply Pelé.

The origins of the nickname are unclear, though it is certain that Pelé has no meaning in Portuguese. The leading theory around the name is that it derived from how the boy would say the name of Bilé, the goalkeeper for Vasco de Gama, his favorite team growing up. Pelé was the son of Brazilian footballer, Dondinho, so he grew up around the game even though the family was impoverished. His first soccer ball was socks stuffed with newspaper and tied with a string. Finally, he was old enough to join the youth team for the local club in his town, Bauru. It was a small club for which his father played, and it became very clear early on that Pelé had talent.

Before he could showcase that talent on the field, however, he needed to come to terms with the nickname that had dominated his life. Edson was just eight years old when a classmate began calling him, Pelé, a moniker that frustrated the young boy. As much as he hated the nickname, the more he got annoyed with classmates calling him Pelé, the more they did it - of course! Eventually, he punched a classmate for calling him the name and earned himself a two-day suspension and a lifetime of being called Pelé.

One reason it bothered him so much is that he truly enjoyed the origins of his name because he was named after American inventor Thomas Edison. But it also created a separation between the person he believed he was – Edson - and the person people perceived him as on and off the field - Pelé. Oftentimes, he refers to Pelé in the third person as if it is a completely different persona to the one that he chooses to use to define himself as a human.

As Pelé was grappling with his identity crisis off the field, there was no crisis at all on the field for the young phenom. He led Bauru to two state championships in Sao Paulo, and he won several futsal (a version of indoor soccer) competitions, including the first one in his region. Pelé had progressed to the point where his games for Bauru were no longer enough of a challenge and his coach, Waldemar de Brito, himself a former member of the Brazilian national team, told Pelé's parents that he needed to look at becoming a professional. That is exactly what Pelé did at the age of 15, traveling to Santos for a tryout with the first team.

In June 1956, Pelé impressed everyone at the club to the point where they signed him to a contract at just 15 years old. He made his debut in September, just short of his 16th birthday, and scored a goal in a 7-1 rout for Santos. By the start of the next season, Pelé had earned a starting spot on the team and proved his worth by leading the league in goals with 36 goals in 29 games in the league. In 1958, Santos won the league on the back of 58 goals for Pelé in just 38 games.

Pelé's performances for his club were more than enough to earn the attention of those at the head of the Brazilian soccer federation. He earned his first cap with the senior national team in 1957 and scored twice in two appearances for his country. He scored nine times in seven games in 1958, including six goals in the knockout stages of the 1958 World Cup, which Brazil won. His domination in the final three games of the tournament caused many of the European powers at the time to pay attention to the 17-year-old.

Over the next four years, the biggest clubs in Europe came to Santos trying to sign away Pelé. Real Madrid, Juventus, and Manchester United were all rebuffed, especially after the Inter Milan incident of 1958. Santos had actually reached a transfer deal with the Italian giants for Pelé's contract, but it was overruled at the last moment after the Brazilian fans revolted. The speculation and pressure built up so much that Brazil's president in 1961, Jânio Quadros, actually declared the then-20-year-old a national treasure just so he couldn't be transferred out of the country.

Santos kept rolling on with Pelé at the top of the formation, taking its domination from the regional Sao Paulo competitions to the national stage. From 1961-65, Pelé led Santos to five straight Brazilian club championships in the newly-formed Campeonato Brasileiro Série A. He led the league in scoring three times in those five years while averaging at least one goal per game every year from 1960 through 1965 for Santos in all competitions. By 1966, Pelé's performances were still elite compared to today's standards but far from the pace that he had set for the first part of his career.

Injuries did play a role in his decline as the physical nature of the game would sometimes counteract his skill. Pelé won the World Cup with Brazil in 1962, but an injury in the second game ended his tournament prematurely with just one goal. Injuries again affected him at the 1966 World Cup where some rough tackles in a game against Portugal forced Pelé off the field.

Yet despite Pelé not being the same dominating figure and Santos losing grip on its stranglehold on Brazilian club soccer, the pair continued to find success. Santos won the regional Campeonato Paulista in 1967, 1968, and 1969 with Pelé leading the way, including 26 goals in 25 games in 1969. This dovetailed perfectly into Pelé's 1970 swan song with the Brazilian national team at the World Cup. He scored four goals in the tournament, including the opening strike in the final against Italy, to leave with three World Cup titles in four appearances at the tournament.

It felt like Pelé's career was winding down after he hit 30 years old, and after four years of declining on-field performance for Santos, Pelé decided to retire in 1974. By the time of this announcement, Pelé had become a worldwide phenomenon the likes no athlete had ever accomplished. His appearance at an exhibition game in Nigeria quite literally stopped a civil war for two days so everyone could attend the match to watch him play! That notoriety and fame were key reasons he was able to have such a captivating second act to his career in the United States.

In 1975, the New York Cosmos of the now-defunct North American Soccer League wanted to make a splash. The club convinced Pelé out of retirement and soccer mania struck the United States like never before. Everywhere the Cosmos went to play, the stadium was sold out and oftentimes above capacity. He played just three seasons in New York, scoring 66 goals in 107 appearances for the team, but Pelé turned around the perception of soccer in the United States. He helped attract bigger European names, other World Cup champions, to come to play in the NASL and help grow the sport.

Yet in 1978, it was time for Pelé to officially hang up the cleats for good, and there was only one way to cap off his legendary career. In front of a sold-out Giants Stadium just outside the limits of New York City, the Cosmos faced off in an exhibition match against Santos. The star-studded list of attendees included Robert Redford, Barbra Streisand, Mick Jagger, and Muhammad Ali, and they all watched Pelé score in the first half for the Cosmos. At halftime, Pelé publicly changed out of the No. 10 Cosmos jersey into a No. 10 Santos jersey at midfield for the second half. He couldn't replicate his goal-scoring feat for his first professional club, but it was a heartfelt moment.

At the end of the game, Pelé again went to midfield, this time to present his final Santos jersey to his first coach in appreciation for all he did for Pelé's career. By this point, there was a massive downpour of rain, leading one Brazilian newspaper to claim that even the skies were crying out of sadness that night.

It is hard to pinpoint exactly how many goals Pelé scored during his career. Many sources claimed he scored more than 1,200 goals in nearly 1,400 games, but that included many friendlies and exhibitions where official statistics aren't counted. Officially, he scored 775 times in 840 games for country and club, but either way, it is a legacy that goes well beyond his impoverished upbringing in the heart of Brazil.

"I don't believe there is such a thing as a 'born' soccer player," Pelé wrote in his autobiography. "Perhaps you are born with certain skills and talents, but quite frankly it seems impossible to me that one is actually born to be an ace soccer player. Success is no accident. It is hard work, perseverance, learning, studying, sacrifice and most of all, love of what you are doing or learning to do."

WILMA RUDOLPH

There are some physical disabilities where it is obvious what is ailing the person. Others like Wilma Rudolph were able to accomplish so much with a physical illness that was difficult to see. For many other people in Rudolph's generation, her diagnosis might have been a death sentence, or at the very least would make becoming an athlete impossible. Yet Rudolph overcame the odds to become a transformational Olympic sprinter who broke so many barriers for the United States.

Wilma Rudolph was born on June 23, 1940, in Tennessee as the 20th of 22 children for her father, who had 14 children from a previous marriage before marrying Wilma's mother. Born prematurely, Rudolph already was facing an uphill battle to survive, but she did just that before various viruses came and ravaged her body. Scarlet fever and pneumonia almost killed her, but she also contracted whooping cough and measles before contracting polio. The polio diagnosis prevented Rudolph from walking normally until she was 11 years old with her left leg left ravaged after she fought off the virus. She was walking with leg braces for five years after contracting polio at four years old then spent two more years with orthopedic shoes before her gait was corrected at 11 years old.

For treatment, Rudolph would take the bus with her mother to make the 50-mile trip to Nashville's Meharry Medical

College from their home in Clarksville, Tennessee. She also received massage four times per week at home from various family members trained by the hospital staff, which helped her regain strength in her left leg. For the first two years of school, Rudolph was forced to be homeschooled due to her illnesses; she didn't attend a regular school until the second grade. Sports, though, were never really an option for Wilma until eighth grade when her legs were strong enough for athletic competition.

Wilma chose to play basketball like her sister, which proved to be a blessing for the young girl. She was talented on the court and earned the nickname "Skeeter" because she flew up and down the court as quickly as a mosquito. But it was actually when she was the referee of a local basketball game that she was discovered by Edward Temple, the track coach at Tennessee State. Whereas many people saw Rudolph as a budding basketball star, Temple saw her speed and movement and thought she could excel on the track.

Still just 14 years old, Rudolph attended a track camp at Tennessee State and eventually became part of the vaunted 'Tigerbelles' track club at the school. After two years of competition with the team, Rudolph was one of the handful of Tigerbelles who Temple took to the Olympic Trials for the 1956 Summer Olympics in Melbourne, Australia. Just qualifying for the team four years after she was able to walk normally would have been impressive enough. But Rudolph always aimed for the best and a disappointing elimination in the second round of the 200-meter dash heats was not going to cut it in Melbourne.

She earned a second chance at a medal in 1956 by running the third leg of the 4x100-meter relay for the United States. The Americans actually ended up tying the existing world record but lost out to record-breaking runs from Australia and Great Britain to finish third. That meant Rudolph returned for her junior year of high school - as an Olympic medalist! It was during that year that Rudolph actually set the goal to improve her performance for the 1960 Olympics in Rome. As she told the *Chicago Tribune* later in life, the fact the bronze didn't shine when she tried to shine it one day after school was enough of a motivating factor.

Before she could get to the 1960 Olympics, however, she became pregnant and gave birth to her daughter, Yolanda. Temple had a rule that forbade mothers from being on his teams at Tennessee State, but he made an exception for Rudolph, who learned self-discipline in the process. After having to run 30 laps for being 30 minutes late to a practice, Rudolph started to take her commitments a bit more seriously. It also helped that she began to mature as well, growing from an 89-pound lanky 16-year-old in Melbourne to a more robust 130-pound 20-year-old in preparation for Italy.

Wilma was much healthier after having her tonsils removed in early 1960, stopping the laundry list of viruses that had made her first two years at Tennessee State as a student that much more difficult. By the time the Olympic Trials came around at Texas Christian University, she was ready to showcase just how special she could be on the track. Rudolph distanced herself easily from the competition in the 100-meter and 200-meter races to qualify for the Olympic Team headed to Rome.

Once the team landed in Italy, there didn't seem to be much that could stop Rudolph from her date with destiny. A small hole in the infield of the track - which Rudolph stepped in the day before the 100-meter heats were set to begin - seemed like it might derail her, but she avoided serious injury. Some ice and a protective strap on her ankle allowed her to win her first heat the equal to the world record of 11.3 seconds to win the semifinal heat. The other thing that could have stopped Rudolph was her notorious poor start. Yet she didn't let the early deficit prevent her from running a wind-aided 11 seconds to win the gold medal, dispatching her nearest rival by three yards in the end.

In the 200-meter dash, Rudolph set the tone early by setting the world record of 23.2 seconds in her first heat. She couldn't quite muster the same speed in the semifinals or the Olympic final, but her time of 24 seconds was more than enough to secure her the gold medal. In fact, her margin of victory was so large that no other sprinter was in the photo when Rudolph crossed the finish line!

Now the 4x100-meter race was the only thing standing between Wilma Rudolph and her destiny of becoming the first American woman to win three track gold medals in a single Olympics. Rudolph anchored the Americans in the relay and helped the United States break the world record in the first heat of the event. Entering the final as the favorite, the U.S. struggled with the baton pass in an early leg and Rudolph took the baton trailing by nearly two meters. In a matter of seconds, Wilma closed the gap and then overtook her challengers, winning the race by a wider margin than she had trailed at the start of her leg. With that third gold medal of the Olympics, Rudolph cemented her status as an American icon.

Rudolph and the rest of the American team participated in several other European meets, and at each one, Wilma received a champion's welcome. Everywhere she went, she was met by applause and a new nickname to describe her running style and determination. In Italy, she was "The

Black Gazelle," and in France, she was "The Black Pearl." The English kept it much simpler, tabbing her "The Tennessee Tornado" as she continued to wow fans with her speed.

Back at home, Rudolph was the center of attention and the cause of a major event in Clarksville, Tennessee history. The celebratory banquet and homecoming parade were the first integrated municipal events in the city's history, allowing everyone in the community to celebrate Rudolph's incredible accomplishments. Yet the Olympics were still an amateur event in the 1960s, so Rudolph was unable to profit from her fame and athletic ability. That was the main reason why she retired from the sport in 1962 at the age of 22 and decided to use her education degree to become a teacher. Before she retired, though, Rudolph won the 1961 James Sullivan Award as the nation's best amateur athlete.

After devoting her life to education, Rudolph found herself in a weird place. Many people expected her to be living a more luxurious life as an Olympic star. Yet she used what means she had to improve the lives of thousands of children with her foundation as well as her own teaching career. That career took her all over the country, but she eventually found her way home to Tennessee in 1992. Shortly after her mother died in 1994, Wilma was diagnosed with brain and throat cancer, and she did not survive the rest of the year.

It would be easy to define Rudolph's life by the illnesses and pain she felt for much of her childhood and then again in the final months of her life. But what she did in a 10-year stretch in the middle was nothing short of incredible and a testament to her character and will to succeed.

"After scarlet fever and whooping cough, I remember I started to get mad about it all," Rudolph said of her childhood. "I went through the stage of asking myself, 'Wilma, what is this existence all about? Is it about being sick all the time? It can't be.' So, I started getting angry about things, fighting back in a new way with a vengeance. I think I started acquiring a competitive spirit right then and there, a spirit that would make me successful in sports later on."

MIKE TYSON

There's fighting out of a poor situation, and then there is FIGHTING out of a poor situation. Anyone who knows the name Mike Tyson knows exactly which type of fighting he chose! A gritty childhood led to a gritty personality inside the ring and some interesting antics outside of it. He might not be the greatest boxer of all time nor is he the greatest heavyweight, yet there is no doubt Tyson's career was iconic, with the highest of highs and lowest of lows.

Mike Tyson was born on June 30, 1966, in Brooklyn, New York into a family that was already on shaky ground. His father left when Mike was just two years old, forcing his mother, brother, and sister to fend for themselves. While growing up in the more dangerous, crime-filled neighborhoods in Brooklyn, Tyson learned how to defend himself. The fights in the neighborhood often left someone with broken bones, if not worse, so it didn't take long for Tyson to develop the power and speed for which he ended up being known in the boxing ring.

Of course, a life filled with fighting on the street also led to a large rap sheet for the young Tyson. He was arrested 38 times by the time he turned 13 years old, and he was committing petty crimes almost daily. Tyson's first fight came when a classmate ripped the head off one of Tyson's beloved pigeons. It was a decisive victory for Tyson and gave him the first inclination that fighting for people's approval felt good to him. Although the petty crimes earned him a long list of charges in his youth, they also led him to the boxing ring.

After being arrested for snatching someone's purse, Tyson was sent to the Tryon School for Boys, where he met Bobby Stewart. The juvenile center's counselor was a former boxer and saw Tyson's raw emotions as something that could be harnessed in the ring. Tyson came to the school at nearly 200 pounds but was able to bench press more than his own body weight, and Stewart took him under his wing and trained him in boxing. After a few months with Stewart, Tyson was transferred into the capable hands of Cus D'Amato.

D'Amato trained former heavyweight champion Floyd Patterson and quickly saw the potential and skill in Tyson. When Tyson was eventually released from Tryon, he moved in with D'Amato in upstate New York. A few years after making the move, Tyson's mother died when he was just 16 years old, and D'Amato became his legal guardian. However, the change in scenery did not lead to a change in behavior for Tyson, who was expelled from high school as a junior and then dropped out.

After his mother's death, Tyson found himself at the start of an explosive amateur boxing career. The heavyweight won the Junior Olympic Championship in both 1981 and 1982, pulverizing his opponents into submission on the way to the titles. He continued his success in 1984 with a victory in the national Golden Gloves tournament, setting up the path for Tyson to represent the United States at the 1984 Summer Olympics in Los Angeles. However, Tyson lost a pair of tight, controversial decisions to Henry Tillman at the Olympic Trials, and then watched his opponent capture the gold medal for the Americans instead.

After the bitter disappointment of 1984, Tyson set his sights on the professional ranks. On March 6, 1985, Tyson made his pro debut against Hector Mercedes and proceeded to make quick work of his opponent with a first-round knockout. He would go on to fight a staggering 15 times in 1985 and he won them all via knockout. Tyson often was able to fight on a short turnaround because he didn't let his bouts last very long. His first 19 victories all came by way of knockout, and many of them came in the first three rounds. Before getting his first title fight, Tyson won 25 of his 27 professional fights via knockout or technical knockout, and 16 of those stoppages were in the first round.

The powerful Tyson was on a meteoric rise and 20 months after his professional debut, he got his chance at the belt. On November 22, 1986, Tyson earned a fight against WBC heavyweight champion Trevor Berbick in Las Vegas. At just 20 years and 145 days old, Tyson became the youngest heavyweight champion ever by stopping Berbick in the second round. Less than four months later, Tyson added the WBA title to his collection with a hard-fought yet decisive win over James Smith that lasted the full 12 rounds. Five months after that fight, Tyson earned another convincing unanimous decision against Tony Tucker to capture the IBF's heavyweight belt.

The underlying issue for Tyson was that his biggest successes came without D'Amato in his corner. The man who invested so much time and energy into a troubled Tyson died in November 1985, leaving Tyson without his father figure. Yet, inside the ring, Tyson was still able to channel D'Amato's teachings and pulverize his opponents with his "peek-a-boo" style that limited the number of punches he absorbed while dishing out his own punishment. His ability to dodge and weave through his opponent's punches at close range while also delivering such devastating blows was the talk of the boxing world and set up a marquee showdown in 1988.

Tyson entered his bout with Michael Spinks as a three-belt heavyweight champion with a perfect 34-0 record. He had won 30 of his bouts by way of knockout and entered the ring in Atlantic City on June 27, 1988, as the biggest name in boxing. The closest competitor to that title was Spinks, who was also undefeated in his career and was The Ring's heavyweight champion. It took just 91 seconds for Tyson to end the fight, collecting a $20 million purse with his dominating performance that left Spinks on the mat.

If he wasn't already the undisputed heavyweight champion, there was no mistaking Tyson as the best boxer in the division after the Spinks fight. However, all of the fame and fortune began to cause issues in Tyson's life. His wife went forward with allegations of physical abuse shortly after the victory and Tyson had a very public divorce from his manager. In August 1988, Tyson broke his hand in a street fight against a fellow fighter then two weeks later, he was found unconscious after crashing his car into a tree. Tyson went from being front-page news for his boxing accomplishments to earning the spotlight for his behavior outside the ring.

The headlines didn't seem to make a difference inside the ring, where Tyson continued to reign supreme for the next two years. He earned a pair of technical knockouts in 1989 to retain his title to set up what should have been another routine matchup for Tyson against James "Buster" Douglas. Tyson was a prohibitive favorite in that fight and looked the part for the early rounds. However, something changed within Tyson after Douglas rose off the mats in the middle rounds after being knocked down.

As he later told *Detail Magazine*, the events of those two years and the tabloid stories affected his love of boxing. Tyson was able to win those two fights in 1989 because he was not only the better fighter but had broken the spirit of his opponents. That wasn't true for Douglas, who came back at Tyson and exploited the champion's apathy in the situation to stun the world with a 10th-round knockout.

Tyson was able to exact some level of revenge in his next fight after the defeat with a first-round knockout of Tillman, the man who beat him twice in 1984 when they were amateurs. He then ended 1990 with another first-round stoppage, taking him that much closer to fighting to reclaim his belts. He won a controversial technical knockout over Donovan "Razor" Ruddock in March 1991, with the referee stopping the fight in the seventh round - much to the crowd's displeasure! Tyson left no doubt three months later with a convincing unanimous decision win over Ruddock to earn a title shot against Evander Holyfield.

That fight with Holyfield would never materialize as a rib injury prevented Tyson from making the first bout. Any rescheduling went out the window when Tyson was arrested and sent to prison on rape charges. When he earned parole in 1995, he returned to the ring with two easy victories, giving him a chance at the WBC title against Frank Bruno. Just 50 seconds into the third round, Tyson earned a technical knockout win to reclaim a belt more than six years after he lost it. Later in 1996, Tyson needed less than two minutes to take down Bruce Seldon for the WBC heavyweight title.

Finally, the Holyfield fight was scheduled for November 1996 and Tyson suffered just his second career loss, with an 11th-round stoppage. The June 1997 rematch is most famous as the fight where Tyson was disqualified for biting off a chunk of Holyfield's ear, sparking the end of Tyson's legendary short career. Tyson was disqualified in the match and lost his boxing license, though it was later reinstated. Tyson would continue to fight for eight more years, and he earned one last title fight in 2002 when he was knocked out by Lennox Lewis in the eighth round.

Outside the ring, Tyson's eccentric personality continued to take center stage as he used his celebrity status. His antics continued to capture the tabloid headlines while his boxing career foundered in the ring. However, things began turning around for Tyson in 2013 as he found his new calling as an actor on screen and stage. In an interview with *Rolling Stone*, Tyson confirmed that he had settled down and found the inner peace he struggled to have for much of his childhood, adolescence, and adulthood. It made sense that Tyson needed to remove himself from the boxing ring and constant fighting to find the peace that might have prevented his boxing career from the beginning.

"I never saw my mother happy with me and proud of me for doing something," Tyson said. "She only knew me as being a wild kid running the streets, coming home with new clothes that she knew I didn't pay for. I never got a chance to talk to her or know about her. Professionally, it had no effect, but it's crushing emotionally and personally."

KURT WARNER

The story of Kurt Warner's rise to fame is one of the most well-known underdog tales of the modern era. From an undrafted grocery clerk to a Super Bowl champion, Warner personifies the never-say-die attitude for which so many athletes strive. Yet what sets Kurt Warner apart from the rest isn't his commitment to the sport nor his perseverance, but his dedication and trust in himself. His belief that things would work out is something many should mirror in their own lives.

Kurt Warner was born on June 22, 1971, in Iowa, which would become the centerpiece of the first half of Warner's story. His parents divorced when Kurt was six years old, and he spent most of his childhood living with his mother along with his brother, Matt. However, his dad remarried shortly after the divorce and Kurt gained a half-brother, also named Matt. The two Matts and Kurt became extremely tight and kindled their love of football together in the yards and streets. Although Warner spent most of his time in the backyard envisioning himself as the quarterback and acted the part while playing with his brothers, he figured his destiny in the sport was in a different position.

Warner showed up to the first day of high school football tryouts as a freshman hoping to play wide receiver for Regis High School. The problem was no one wanted to try out to play quarterback, so the coach lined up everyone and had them throw the ball as far as they could. Much to Warner's chagrin, he won the contest and became the team's quarterback. In his mind, the path to the NFL was not bright for quarterbacks from Iowa, and so he felt as though his dream died that day. That seemed especially true considering just how raw Warner was at the position, particularly when it came to the tackles.

Having grown up as a receiver known for juking out of tackles and scoring touchdowns, it took Warner a while to learn how to absorb the hit and make the play. He spent much of his first few games dodging the pressure and running himself, focusing less on his receivers and throwing them the ball and more on evading the pass rushers. Warner's high school coach invented a drill specifically designed to force Kurt into facing his fears, and that drill helped Warner become an all-state quarterback.

Out of Regis, Warner earned a shot with the Northern Iowa football team but was a backup for the Panthers for his first four years. He finally earned a chance to lead UNI in 1993, his redshirt senior year, and he took the then-Gateway Conference by storm. He was the league's Offensive Player of the Year and first-team all-conference quarterback while leading the Panthers to the conference title. Yet it wasn't enough for Warner to get drafted in the 1994 NFL Draft.

Warner did get a chance in the NFL with the Green Bay Packers, who signed Warner as a free agent. However, it was a short-lived trial in a crowded quarterback room, and Warner was released before the 1994 season. Without a place to play football, Warner took a job as a graduate assistant with the Northern Iowa football team while also stocking shelves at the local grocery store during overnight hours. It was an exhausting routine for Warner, who played dad during the day in addition to his job at UNI and managed to sneak in a workout during the afternoon to stay sharp for his NFL opportunity while also stocking shelves when most other people slept.

No NFL chance came in 1995 for Warner, but he did get an offer to play professional football in his home state with the Iowa Barnstormers of the Arena Football League. Warner may be the most famous alumni of the AFL, but he also earned plenty of plaudits during his short stint in the league. He was twice named the league's first-team all-star quarterback after he led the Barnstormers to the championship game in 1996 and 1997. In those two seasons, he combined to throw 140 touchdowns to just 29 interceptions across 28 starts while completing more than 63 percent of his passes.

After a second consecutive strong season in the AFL, Warner got his next NFL chance thanks to the Chicago

Bears. The Bears called to schedule a workout with Warner in the summer of 1997, but he forgot when he booked the session that he was getting married that weekend. He postponed it to the following week - but he was going to be on his honeymoon in Jamaica then! So, he again asked to reschedule, and the Bears obliged. As the couple was set to travel home for Warner's workout, a bug - most likely a spider - bit Warner's elbow and his throwing arm became inflamed to about the size of a grapefruit. Out of commission, Warner had to pass on what might have been his final NFL chance.

Just a few months earlier in late 1996, Warner had his first look at an NFL job when he received a phone call out of the blue from Al Luginbill, a head coach in NFL Europe. He was curious if Warner was interested in playing for him with the Amsterdam Admirals for the 1997 season, suggesting he could use his position to try and gain another shot at the NFL. Warner said he would join the team in Amsterdam if Luginbill could find a team to also invite Warner to training camp. When no one was willing to offer Warner that elusive invitation, Warner declined to play in Europe.

Yet Luginbill didn't quit on Warner and called him back the next year with the same offer, and Warner offered the same conditions. Luginbill called 12 different teams and received the same polite rejection, but the 13th team he tried agreed to offer Warner that trip to training camp. That was, of course, dependent on a workout with the St. Louis Rams, which felt like a foregone conclusion for him. Yet Warner had what he deemed the worst workout of his life and called his wife in tears thinking he had lost his final shot at playing in the NFL. St. Louis saw some potential, though, and in late 1997, signed Warner to a futures contract with the expectation that he would also play for the Admirals in 1998. The signing was so low on the radar for the Rams and fans that the *St. Louis Post Dispatch* actually misidentified Warner's alma mater in their short story on the signing!

Warner did what he does best and led the league in passing yards and touchdowns in NFL Europe. Entering training camp with confidence, Warner made it to the final day of roster cuts in a battle for the third-string quarterback job. Much like the Rams took a chance on Warner after that terrible audition workout, they bet on his talent by keeping him as the third-string quarterback. Of course, he barely saw the field in 1998 and was a great unknown when he was promoted to back-up behind the newly-signed Trent Green for the 1999 season.

For much of his life, Warner made his own luck happen to put him in a position to play in the NFL, but his career needed a boost. Although no one roots for an injury, Green's torn ACL in the preseason ahead of the 1999 season was the break Warner needed. The Rams turned to him as their starter, hoping just to survive the year until Green was ready to return - but St. Louis didn't just survive, it thrived. With Warner at the helm and a talented group of skilled players around him, the "Greatest Show on Turf" was born within Mike Martz's offense.

The same quarterback who the Rams left unprotected in the 1999 expansion draft was suddenly making NFL defenses look foolish. Warner threw three touchdown passes in his first start and 14 over the course of his first four games, leading St. Louis to a perfect 4-0 mark. He would end the season with 4,353 passing yards and league-leading 41 passing touchdowns as well as the label NFL MVP. The Rams went 13-3 that season on the way to the top seed in the NFC for the postseason. They rolled past Minnesota in the divisional round then snuck past Tampa Bay in the NFC title game to reach the franchise's first Super Bowl in 20 years. In the biggest game of his career, Warner threw for 414 yards and two touchdowns to bring a Super Bowl title to St. Louis and earn Super Bowl MVP honors.

It was the type of Hollywood script that would never get approved for being too unrealistic, yet that is exactly what happened to Warner. After leading the Rams to the title, he signed a seven-year contract worth $46.5 million, including an $11.5 million signing bonus. This came on the heels of making just $250,000 in base salary in 1999 with an extra half million dollars in bonuses. In his first three seasons as the starting quarterback, Warner was 35-8 with 12,612 passing yards and 98 passing touchdowns while completing 67.2 percent of his passes. He led the NFL in passing yards in 2001 while leading the Rams to a second Super Bowl appearance in three years. However, he also led the league in completion percentage in all three years and led the NFL in passing touchdowns in the two Super Bowl campaigns. Plus, he took home a pair of NFL MVP titles in that span as well.

The 2002 season got off to a rough start for Warner, and a broken hand sidelined him for an extended period. He never let the injury fully heal, however, which cost him his starting job in 2003 when he had a fumbling issue caused by his lack of grip on the ball. After being cut by the Rams, he immediately signed with the Giants as an intended mentor to Eli Manning, but after being benched early in the season, Warner decided to void his contract at the end of 2004.

There was hope for Warner in 2005 when he signed with the Arizona Cardinals, but he struggled to stay healthy and make an impact on the field. Just when it felt like Warner was about to fizzle out of the league, buoyed by the magical three-year run, he found yet another gear for his career. He impressed in 2007 when coming on in relief for Matt Leinart and then usurped the USC quarterback for the job ahead of the 2008 season. He completed two-thirds of his passes in 2008 and threw for more than 4,500 yards to lead the Cardinals to the playoffs for the first time in a decade.

Similar to his run with the Rams in 1999, Warner felt like a man of destiny during the 2008 postseason. He led the Cardinals to the Super Bowl for the first time in franchise history after throwing four touchdowns and no interceptions against Philadelphia in the NFC Championship Game. Unlike the fairy-tale ending in 1999, Arizona fell short in 2008 to the Pittsburgh Steelers, but it set up a remarkable 2009 season. For the first time since the mid-1970s, Arizona made the playoffs in consecutive years thanks in large part to Warner. However, an early injury in the divisional round ended Warner's season and career just a week after a near-perfect performance against the Packers. In that first postseason game in 2009, Warner completed 29 of 33 passes for 379 yards and five touchdowns to become the first since the AFL-NFL merger to throw for five touchdowns in the playoffs twice.

There are a lot of unknowns with Warner's career, and several moments when a little bit of luck helped him get over the finish line. Yet Warner was always prepared when those breaks showed up, and no one made more of their opportunities than the former Northern Iowa quarterback.

When he was healthy, Warner was among the best quarterbacks in the league for roughly a decade, which is not something anyone who spent time stocking grocery stores after college probably should be able to say.

"For those who have witnessed my career from the outside, you will undoubtedly use the milestones Super Bowls, MVPs, and of course tonight as the defining moments of my career," Warner said in his Hall of Fame induction speech. "But if there's one thing that this process has revealed, it's that those pinnacle accomplishments on the field were simply byproducts of the moments that would lay the foundation of the man who stands here this evening. Moments that few have heard about, and even fewer witnessed. Moments that, no matter how insignificant they seemed at the time, would become the backdrop of my story. Moments which would shape my character and set the stage for one unforgettable journey."

SERENA WILLIAMS

When athletes face adversity, it isn't always in the traditional sense of the word. Serena Williams was remarkably healthy throughout her entire career, and she was able to balance both being a kid with being a tennis phenomena. One might even argue that she was extremely fortunate that her parents went out of their way to support her and her sister in the manner that they did. But that discounts what it actually meant to be a powerful, Black female icon in her era, and the torment she faced on her road to stardom and success.

Serena Williams was born in Michigan on September 26, 1981, but she moved to Compton, California at a young age. It was there that Williams was first introduced to tennis, and it became an instant passion. Her first coach was Richard Williams and it became apparent quickly that both Serena and her sister, Venus, had talent. Both of them shared their father's pursuit of perfection, Venus being far more the perfectionist than Serena. By the time Serena turned nine, the family was on the move again, this time to West Palm Beach, Florida to train with Rick Macci.

While at Macci's academy, Serena blossomed into one of the top-rated junior tennis players in the country. She was 46-3 at the under-10 level and a dominant force on the south Florida junior tennis circuit. However, while Serena was playing on the court, she was subjected to her first bit of racism from the parents of her opponents. Within a year of moving to Florida, Serena stopped playing national junior tennis tournaments because of the hurtful comments from the White parents. Williams' father claimed at the time that he wanted his daughter to develop more slowly and focus on his academics, but also admitted the racist remarks did play a role.

Williams remained at Macci's academy for four years until her father decided to resume as his daughters' main coach once again. In 1995, Williams was scheduled to play in the Bank of the West Classic in California along with her sister, Venus, but the age restrictions on the WTA Tour barred her from competing. Serena filed a brief lawsuit trying to gain entry as a wildcard, but she withdrew the suit and settled for a professional debut in a lower-tiered event in Quebec, Canada.

The odyssey to her first professional match was intense. She and her father missed their flight in Philadelphia and stopped in four airports on their way to the tournament. In the mix-up, Serena lost her rackets, and she arrived too late to actually practice on the courts before her match! Whether it was the travel issues or her lack of matches in tournament settings, Williams looked far from a teenage phenomena in her 6-1, 6-1 defeat to Anne Miller. After her debut, Serena did not play in any tournaments in 1996 as she prepared for her WTA Tour debut at the age of 16.

Serena landed in Palm Springs, California in March 1997 to get another chance at playing on the WTA Tour. However, she lost in the opening qualifying round and did not play another professional event until August. In that tournament in Los Angeles, Williams won her first professional match with a 6-1, 6-4 win over Amanda Basica in the opening qualifying round. Yet she lost in the third and final qualifying stage, falling short of the main draw in her home state.

Serena played a tournament in Switzerland in October and advanced to the second qualifying round before stumbling, but that first main draw match was just around the corner. The next week in Moscow, Williams finally broke through and qualified for the main draw with three straight-set victories in qualifying. However, the success was short-lived as she lost in straight sets in the opening round.

The following week, Serena earned a wildcard entry into the Ameritech Cup in Chicago for what would be her second main-draw match. Yet that November week in the Windy City was a showcase of the potential the young Williams had in her game. In the first round of the tournament, she took down Elena Likhovtseva in straight sets for her first win in a professional tournament's main draw. She didn't stop there, however, and went on to upset world No. 7, Mary Pierce, 6-3, 7-6(3) to advance to the quarterfinals. There, Serena overcame dropping the first set to defeat fourth-ranked Monica Seles, 4-6, 6-1, 6-1 to advance to the semifinals against Lindsay Davenport.

Although Williams' run ended with a loss to Davenport, Serena's final tournament of 1997 sent a message to the tennis community that she was ready to be a force on the tour. She proved as much in January 1998 when she debuted with a run to the semifinals in an Australian Open warmup event in Sydney. In the quarterfinals in Sydney, Williams defeated Davenport in three sets for her third top-10 victory in two months. Serena's debut at a Grand Slam event began with a victory over sixth-seeded Irina Spirlea, but a second-round matchup against Venus left the younger sister with a 6-7, 1-6 defeat.

That tournament in Sydney was the last time Williams had to qualify for a tournament after moving into the top 50 following her appearance at the Australian Open. She entered the 1998 French Open as the 27th-ranked player in the world and advanced to the fourth round on the clay. She was forced to retire in the third round of Wimbledon that year and also fell in the third round of the U.S. Open in 1998 all the while still searching for her first final on the tour as a singles player.

Williams found plenty of success with Venus on the doubles court. She was a semi-finalist with her sister in Chicago in

1997 while she was also making her run in the singles bracket. The pair won a doubles title in Oklahoma in 1998 then finished the year with a championship in Switzerland as well. Serena was also adept at winning mixed doubles titles at the Grand Slam, capturing the championships at Wimbledon and the U.S. Open with Max Mirnyi after falling in the final of the French Open with Luis Lobo to Venus and her partner, Justin Gimelstob.

Serena was already a consistent top-25 player by the time she arrived in Paris in late February 1999. She was coming off a third-round exit in the Australian Open when she began her tournament in France with an easy win over Asa Svensson. She then easily handled her next three opponents, all of them French, to reach the first final of her career against another Frenchwoman, Amelie Mauresmo. The two split the first two sets then Serena powered down in the tiebreaker to emerge with her first title.

Proving to win is contagious, Williams won her second singles title the next month with a three-set victory over Steffi Graf in Palm Springs for her first Tier I victory. She then advanced to the final of her next tournament but lost to Venus in three sets. Serena also won a Tier II event in Los Angeles that summer. However, she still failed to advance to the fourth round of a Grand Slam event since the 1998 French Open.

After winning in Los Angeles, Williams entered the 1999 U.S. Open as the seventh seed and the No. 6 player in the world after hovering around No. 10 for much of the year. A pair of straight-set victories to kick off the tournament got the momentum flowing, but Serena dropped the first set of the third-round match against Kim Clijsters. She battled back to take down the Belgian and then put herself in a similar position in the fourth round against Conchita Martinez. Williams dominated the final two sets to reach a Grand Slam quarterfinal for the first time and had to face Monica Seles. Another first-set loss was followed by victories in the second and third sets to send Serena to the semifinals. She still went three sets with Lindsey Davenport, but actually won the first set this time then rallied from a poor second set to capture the match.

That left just a match with top-ranked Martina Hingis for her first Grand Slam title. Williams had won two of the three previous meetings with Hingis in 1999 with both of her wins coming in the semifinals. Hingis had won five Grand Slams already and was dominant on the hard courts with three wins in the Australian Open and a 1-1 record in the U.S. Open finals. Yet Williams was undeterred and took down the Swiss champion 6-3, 7-6 (4) for her first Grand Slam singles title, adding to the doubles titles she won with Venus that year in New York as well.

The sisters eventually teamed up to win 14 doubles titles in Grand Slams, becoming just the fifth duo ever to win all four Grand Slams together with a victory in the 2001 Australian Open. The Williams sisters were a perfect 14-0 in doubles finals as well, with six wins at Wimbledon, four at the Australian Open and then two each at the U.S. Open and French Open. The pair also won three Olympic gold medals together, teaming up for the titles in 2000 in Sydney, 2008 in Beijing, and 2012 in London.

As a singles player, Serena was still trying to find her groove, especially with all the attention that came as a Grand Slam champion. She was less than a month shy of her 18th birthday when she won the U.S. Open, becoming just the second Black woman to win a singles title in a Grand Slam event. The 2000 and 2001 seasons were successful by most metrics, with a plethora of titles and deep runs befitting her top-10 ranking. Yet from Wimbledon in 2000 through to the U.S. Open in 2001, Williams went six straight Grand Slams reaching the quarterfinals without a title. The closest she came was the 2001 U.S. Open when she lost to Venus in the final in straight sets.

That set up an impactful 2002 that started off rocky as an injury in a warmup tournament forced Williams to withdraw from the Australian Open. She won titles on her return in Arizona and Miami, defeating the three top-ranked players in the world on the way to that Miami championship. Serena entered the 2002 French Open as the third seed after rising to No. 3 in the rankings with a win at the Italian Open. She exacted a measure of revenge by defeating Venus to win the French Open and move up to No. 2 in the world. The Williams sisters meeting in the Grand Slam finals became a theme over the next year and a half. Serena and Venus faced off for the title in a Grand Slam five times in a six-Slam stretch, and Serena won all of those matchups. That includes the 2002 Wimbledon Championships when Serena climbed to the top spot in the world rankings for the first time.

With her victory in the 2003 Australian Open over Venus, Serena completed what is now known as the "Serena Slam" as the holder of all four Grand Slam titles at one time. She lost out on the French Open title in 2003, but she defended her Wimbledon title for the sixth Grand Slam of her career. With her ascension to the No. 1 overall ranking, Williams was at the top of her game, and no one could compete with that level of success. She was ranked No. 1 in the world for a staggering 319 weeks during her career, including a record-setting 186 consecutive weeks at one point.

In the biggest events, Serena played some of her finest tennis as well, with 23 Grand Slam titles, the most of anyone in the Open Era and second-most all-time. Her 23-

10 record in finals fell one short of Chris Evert's 34 appearances in the final and Williams was a remarkable 33-7 in the semifinals. No one won more than Serena's 367 Grand Slam matches - though no other player had even played 367 Grand Slam matches! Serena stands alone with her seven Australian Open titles and is tied with Evert with six U.S. Open championships. Williams also won seven times at Wimbledon, which is good enough for second-most all-time.

By 2012, the only thing missing from Serena's legacy was an Olympic gold medal in singles. Serena didn't play singles in 2000 and she had to withdraw from the tournament in 2004 due to injury, so her first chance came in 2008. Seeded fourth, Williams lost in a tight three-set match in the quarterfinals, coming home emptyhanded in singles medals. In 2012, Serena was seeded fourth yet again but didn't leave anything to chance this time. She dropped just eight games in her final four matches of the tournament, steamrolling Maria Sharapova 6-0, 6-1 in the final to capture her gold medal.

Looking back on her career, it isn't hard to see how talented Williams was on the tennis court. Between her fiery personality that led to a few noteworthy outbursts, there was a dedicated professional who strived to be at the top of her game consistently. However, Williams also took a nontraditional route to the top by skipping junior tournaments and learning how to be a professional on the spot. Many might have questioned the idea when Serena first started on the WTA Tour, but no one can doubt the results it has achieved.

"Growing up I wasn't the richest, but I had a rich family in spirit," Williams said after winning the 2015 Australian Open. "Standing here with 19 championships is something I never thought would happen. I went on a court just with a ball and a racket and with hope."

CONCLUSION

These last 12 chapters have showcased just how many different challenges people can overcome to accomplish their dreams. All of the athletes featured in this book had incredible obstacles they needed to overcome to fulfill their fantasies. You can use this book as motivation not only to improve yourself on the field but to make yourself a better person in life. The beauty of these stories is not in the athletic accomplishments but in how these athletes model their behavior that will help you for the rest of your life. Although all of these people had incredible athletic skills, more importantly, their stories highlight the life skills you need to be successful.

The most obvious common theme in this book is perseverance, and that is very necessary. It's not just understanding there will be challenges but learning how to get back up when you trip and fall. Kurt Warner didn't give up after he was cut by the Packers and didn't play in the NFL for four years, nor did he when his chance at a tryout was interrupted by the spider bite. Lionel Messi didn't let his size dictate what he could and could not do on the soccer field, Bethany Hamilton didn't let her arm being bitten off stop her, nor did Wilma Rudolph let polio deny her from becoming an all-world sprinter.

Yet with perseverance comes dedication and commitment. It is impossible to persevere through adversity without being dedicated and committed to the objective. It's the shining light at the end of the tunnel of work that keeps people driving for better results. Josh Allen didn't settle for being a good junior college quarterback; he pushed himself to be a great Division I quarterback and then an excellent NFL quarterback. Simone Biles didn't let her past accomplishments define her and instead proved to herself that she could be better and more dominant. Serena Williams continued to battle back and dominated long after her former peers retired and a new, younger crop of players arrived.

Most crucially, however, we hope these 12 stories showed you that not everything is as easy as people make it out to be. Yes, LeBron James makes playing basketball look effortless. Pelé made it look like he was born with a soccer ball at his feet that he could dribble at will. Mike Tyson was as dominant of a fighter as there was in boxing, finishing his opponents early in bouts. Yet you saw how all of them faced incredible challenges and had to learn a lot of lessons just to find themselves in the position to be global superstars.

These 12 chapters should definitely inspire you, but they should also serve as a teaching tool as well. Hopefully, you're ready to face those fears and challenge the world with your incredible drive for success after reading these stories.

Made in United States
North Haven, CT
01 March 2023

33379724R00068